TAKING THE REINS

16/4/2012

The Myth of Arab Piracy in the Gulf

The Fragmentation of the Omani Empire

The British Occupation of Aden

My Early Life

TAKING THE REINS
THE CRITICAL YEARS, 1971–1977

Sultan bin Muhammad al-Qasimi

Translated from the Arabic by Dr Ahmed Ali

Edited by Dr Colyn R. Davey and Dr Khaled Hroub

BLOOMSBURY

LONDON · BERLIN · NEW YORK · SYDNEY

First published in 2012

First published in 2010 in Arabic as *Hadeeth al zakira* by Al Qasimi Publications

Copyright © 2010 by Sultan bin Muhammad al-Qasimi
Translation copyright © 2012 by Sultan bin Muhammad al-Qasimi

The moral right of the author has been asserted

All images reproduced in this book are from the author's private collection

Bloomsbury Publishing Plc
50 Bedford Square
London
WC1B 3DP

www.bloomsbury.com

Bloomsbury Publishing, London, Berlin, New York and Sydney
A CIP catalogue record for this book is available from the British Library

ISBN 978 1 4081 8017 4

10 9 8 7 6 5 4 3 2 1

Typeset by Hewer Text UK Ltd, Edinburgh
Printed in Dubai by Oriental Press

Contents

Foreword

O N 2 DECEMBER 1971 THE United Arab Emirates was founded, initially comprising six independent emirates: Abu Dhabi, Dubai, Sharjah, 'Ajman, Umm al-Quwain and al-Fujairah. On 25 January 1972, I was elected Ruler of Sharjah. A seventh and final emirate, Ras al-Khaimah, joined the Federation on 10 February 1972.

Over the six-year period covered in this book, rapid developments took place in both Sharjah specifically and in the United Arab Emirates as a whole. Life changed from division to unity, from fear to safety, from unemployment to the provision of dignified career opportunities, from ignorance to education and knowledge, from rejection of others to acceptance and accommodation of them, and from seeking aid from donors to becoming donors ourselves.

Where the events narrated in this volume run in a chronological order, in some cases I found it more helpful to pay more attention to the subject matter in order to keep the links with other events than staying to a strict chronology.

I pray to Allah, Almighty, to bless this present work of mine, that it might prove to be a useful source of information to the sons and daughters of the Emirates, for '*He is my Lord upon whom I depend, and to whom I shall return*'.

I want to take this opportunity to express my sincere and heartfelt thanks to the Editor-in-Chief of *al-Ittihād* (the Union) newspaper and all its staff members, as well as all the employees of the National Centre for Documentation and Research of the Ministry of Presidential Affairs.

Shaikh Sultan bin Muhammad al-Qasimi,
February 2012

I

*The Emergence of the
United Arab Emirates*

ON 24 JANUARY 1972, FORTY-FIVE days after the foundation of the United Arab Emirates, my brother, Shaikh Khalid bin Muhammad al-Qasimi – who, up to that day, had been the Ruler of Sharjah and a Member of the Federation's Supreme Council – was assassinated.[1]

Sad Days

Wednesday 26 January 1972 was the day of the Eid. After the Eid prayer, prayers were offered for my late brother. The crowds then followed the funeral procession headed by the Vice-President, HH Shaikh Rashid bin Sa'id al-Maktoum, and Ruler of Dubai, and Their Highnesses, the members of the Supreme Council. However, HH Shaikh Rashid bin Humaid al-Nu'aimi, Ruler of 'Ajman, was not able to be there as he was performing *Hajj*

---

[1] For further details on the circumstances surrounding the assassination, see author's book, *My Early Life*, London: Bloomsbury, 2011.

(pilgrimage) in Saudi Arabia at the time. Throughout the funeral, the voices of the crowds were raised in *du'aa* (supplications to Allah) for the deceased, added to the tears of the men, women and children present. My late brother was very popular and well regarded as a ruler by all.

For the following seven days, I received many groups of people from all over the Emirates and the rest of the Arab states who came to pay their condolences. During this period of mourning, the United Arab Emirates flag was lowered for forty days in honour of my brother.

A Brave Stand

On Wednesday 2 February 1972 I held a meeting with the senior officials in the Sharjah government to address the country's situation in light of recent developments. I assured them that, under the supervision of the Ministry of the Interior, a special commission had been formed to investigate the killing of my brother, and to bring his murderers to justice.[2]

As people throughout the Emirates were shaken by the assassination of one of its rulers only a few weeks after the formation of the Federation, HH Shaikh Muhammad bin Rashid al-Maktoum, Minister of Defence, also made a statement that left a profoundly reassuring impression on all: 'The Federal Armed Forces are on full alert to deter any attempt that might target the unity and solidarity of the Arab Emirates,' he said. 'The United Arab Emirates is capable of thwarting any

---

[2] See previous footnote.

4

aggression against its territories. We advise those who may be thinking of infringing on the sovereignty of the United Arab Emirates to think twice before embarking on such a reckless act, as we will be responding with an iron resolve. Our Federal Army is fully prepared to respond aggressively to any and all attempts to undermine the Federation and its independence. Every step the Federal government takes is carefully thought out; security and stability are already well established and prevail throughout the United Arab Emirates,' he added.

Ras al-Khaimah Joins the Federation

On Sunday 6 February 1972, HH Shaikh Rashid bin Sa'id al-Maktoum, Ruler of Dubai and Vice-President of the United Arab Emirates, approached HH Shaikh Zayed bin Sultan Al Nahyan, President of the United Arab Emirates, regarding Ras al-Khaimah joining the Federation. Prior to this meeting, Shaikh Abdullah al-Fadl, Saudi representative to the United Arab Emirates, had been mediating between Shaikh Saqr bin Muhammad al-Qasimi, Ruler of Ras al-Khaimah, and HH Shaikh Rashid bin Sa'id al-Maktoum. After the meeting, Shaikh Zayed decided that Ras al-Khaimah should be allowed to join the Federation, if he managed to talk me into accepting Ras al-Khaimah's membership. Sharjah's acceptance was necessary since, at the time of forming the Federation in 1971, Ras al-Khaimah had hoped to negotiate joining terms that would have had adverse effects on Sharjah's position.

As a meeting of the Supreme Council had been arranged for 9 February 1972, I arrived in Abu Dhabi the previous day.

However, the meeting was postponed, without prior notice, until 10 February. On the evening of the day I arrived, the President sent a message requesting that I meet with him at al-Bahr Palace regarding an important matter. So, after the *Maghrib* (sunset) prayer, I headed for the meeting. At the palace, the Head of Ceremonies led me to Shaikh Zayed. I found him sitting on a carpet laid for him under some palm trees whose branches were dangling on the ground. He was with HH Shaikh Rashid bin Sa'id al-Maktoum, his Vice-President.

After they welcomed me and seated me between them, HH Shaikh Zayed commented: 'The consequences of Ras al-Khaimah being outside the Federation could be dire, and so I am asking you, Shaikh Sultan, to accept our invitation to Shaikh Saqr bin Muhammad al-Qasimi, Ruler of Ras al-Khaimah, to join the United Arab Emirates; I am prepared to meet all the demands that Sharjah may make.'

'I fully agree with both of you that if Ras al-Khaimah remains out of the Federation there could be grave consequences, and that its admission would add to the strength of the Federation. As for making demands on you in return for my approval of the principle of strengthening the Federation, I shall refrain from doing so, Your Highness. This goes totally against my nature and principles,' I said.

Shaikh Rashid bin Sa'id al-Maktoum then turned to Shaikh Zayed and said: 'Zayed, this is the Sultan that I have told you about. I shall leave you both together as I need to return to Dubai.' I still have no idea what HH Shaikh Rashid bin Sa'id al-Maktoum had said about me that evening.

On Thursday 10 February 1972, Ras al-Khaimah officially joined the State of the United Arab Emirates.

Iran's Shah Visits Abu Musa Island

The news was circulated that, on 6 March 1972, the Shah of Iran would pay a visit to Abu Musa Island. For such a visit to take place would have been a slap in the face of the United Arab Emirates, for historically the island belongs to Sharjah and is now under the sovereignty of the UAE against false Iranian claims.

The British, on their part, requested that such a visit be postponed until a later date, and suggested that, in the meantime, perhaps the Shah should visit Sharjah first or at least exchange communications about Abu Musa Island prior to his visit there.

The British also confirmed with me that the Shah's plan seemed completely contradictory to the policy that had been agreed upon with the late Shaikh Khalid bin Muhammad al-Qasimi regarding Iran. From my side, I expected a strong reaction from the Arab world that would bring the problem of the islands in the Gulf to a head.

Later on I came to learn that Mr Bob Burns, Sharjah Police Commander, had obtained the following report from the British Consulate in Dubai, which in turn had received it from Tehran on 29 March 1972. The report read: 'According to the morning newspapers, the Iranian Chief of Staff announced that the Shah had visited the Island of Abu Musa the day before. He made his way from the island of Qays, where he had been, to Abu Musa.'

The papers also said that the Shah had received a tumultuous welcome from the Abu Musa inhabitants, and that he had listened to reports from Iranian locals regarding the military garrisons there and the special plans to develop the economy of Abu Musa. In addition, he inspected the Iranian fleet preparations and issued a number of decrees for the improvement of the standard of living of the seven hundred Abu Musa residents before returning to Qays.

Furthermore, the Iranian newspaper *Kayhan* published reports regarding special plans to construct a water barrier, a hospital and a school and an article about a new market that was already in operation. The newspaper went on to report that two task groups dealing with the prevention of malaria were already working there, and that additional steps for the development of activities relating to fishing and trade on Abu Musa Island were already in place.

Upon further inquiry, however, the Abu Musa inhabitants denied having had any talks with the Shah. According to them, all that happened was that he had driven by in a military vehicle.

This incident occurred but not a single word about it was mentioned in the Abu Dhabi media; and not a single word of protest was raised by any Arab state.

President of UAE Enhances Internal and External Relations

On 29 March 1972, HH Shaikh Zayed bin Sultan Al Nahyan, President of the United Arab Emirates, started a ten-day tour of the Emirates.

On Friday 14 April, I received HH Shaikh Zayed in Sharjah. His helicopter arrived from Khawaneej in Dubai where he was staying during the tour, and it landed in the Batha'a (the Large Wadi) in front of the farm of HH Shaikh Zayed in the Dhaid area of Sharjah where I had been waiting for his reception with Sharjah dignitaries drawn from the ranks of both Bedouins and city dwellers. After Shaikh Zayed had conversed with them and they had left, I stayed with him for about an hour. Our discussion focused on the trial of the assassins of the late Shaikh Khalid bin Muhammad al-Qasimi. In addition, we addressed a variety of political issues in relation to the other Rulers and we spoke to various groups of the locals wherever Shaikh Zayed went.

By way of a gift, HH Shaikh Zayed also gave funds for the construction of:

- 400 local houses;
- 10 mosques;
- 5 medical clinics;
- the digging of 200 water wells; and
- the purchase of 200 water pumps.

Shaikh Zayed told me that his visit had far exceeded his expectations. However, he was saddened when he talked with the locals who had expected a Federation that would benefit them directly. His tone of voice made it clear to me that he felt it was his responsibility to take personal command of such matters.

At the end of February 1972, HH Shaikh Zayed paid a series of important visits to Sudan, Libya and Syria. His meetings with Presidents Nimeiry, Gaddafi and Hafiz al-Asad respectively were centred on achieving close ties of communication with all the

9

Arab countries. He believed that this was not only a national necessity, but was also the only way to form a unified front in the face of Israeli aggression, particularly after the 1967 war and Israel's occupation of more Arab land.

The visits of HH Shaikh Zayed to those Arab countries also revealed the great esteem that the United Arab Emirates enjoyed in the region, in addition to the high level of respect and admiration that other Arab countries had for the economic, social and cultural progress made by the United Arab Emirates in such a short period of time. It was also clear that everyone admired and supported the open-door policy led by Shaikh Zayed in support of Arab causes.

The official statements made after Shaikh Zayed's visits to Khartoum, Tripoli and Damascus were not of the conventional type usually made after visits of heads of states to other countries. On the contrary, they truly expressed the Arab and national values and principles that Shaikh Zayed wholeheartedly believed in. Those statements had emphasised a full understanding of the scale of the confrontation with Israel even for those Arab countries not surrounding Israel. They also included full support of the right of the Palestinian people to return to their home country and their acts of resistance, calling for a strategy towards unifying the Palestinians. In these statements, steps were taken to establish a Federation incorporating the Arab republics which, together with the United Arab Emirates, were declared as aiming at achieving a larger unity that would incorporate all Arab countries from 'the Atlantic Ocean to the Arabian Gulf'.

First President to Visit the United Arab Emirates

For the purpose of accomplishing the policies of the United Arab Emirates that aimed at establishing close relations with the world in general and with Arab countries in particular, HH the President of the State invited His Excellency, the President of Sudan, Jaafar Numeiry, to visit the United Arab Emirates. The invitation was received positively and on 23 April President Numairi came to Abu Dhabi, where he was welcomed with enthusiastic official recognition and public acclaim.

During a sitting of the Sharjah General Council, President Nimeiry presented me with the Sudanese Sash of Honour. Mr Nabil Murad, Deputy-Director of Protocol at the Khartoum People's Palace, delivered a speech on behalf of the Sudanese President in honour of the occasion. He said:

> In appreciation of the great role you have assumed on behalf of Sharjah and the United Arab Emirates to achieve progress for – and the welfare of – its citizens; and by way of marking this auspicious meeting in response to the generous invitation by HH Shaikh Zayed bin Sultan, it is my pleasure, on behalf of the people and government of the Democratic Republic of Sudan, to present the Sudanese Sash of Honour to HH Shaikh Sultan bin Muhammad al-Qasimi, Ruler of Sharjah, in the ardent hope that he will accept it.

President Nimeiry also presented the Sudanese Sash of Honour to:

- Shaikh Rashid bin Humaid al-Nu'aimi, Ruler of 'Ajman;
- Shaikh Saqr bin Muhammad al-Qasimi, Ruler of Ras al-Khaimah;
- Shaikh Ahmad bin Rashid al-Mu'alla, Ruler of Umm al-Quwain;
- Shaikh Khalifah bin Zayed Al Nahyan, Crown Prince of Abu Dhabi: and
- Shaikh Maktoum bin Rashid al-Maktoum, Crown Prince of Dubai.

British Anger

In the light of the active regional role, visits and statements made by the United Arab Emirates President, Shaikh Zayed bin Sultan Al Nahyan, the British – together with the Shah of Iran and Iran's Foreign Minister, Khalatbary – became very angry. In particular, they were very concerned with regard to the fact that Shaikh Zayed was establishing relations with countries with which neither Britain nor Iran wanted him to have anything to do. This anger was reflected in the correspondence of Mr Patrick Wright, Head of the Middle East Department in the British Foreign Office, to his superiors on 31 May 1972:[3]

> In the field of foreign affairs the President[4] has been far less successful. We greatly deplored the communiqués issued after his visits to Sudan, Libya and Syria, and the communiqué

---

[3] This text is an exact transcription of the original document.
[4] Referring to HH Shaikh Zayed bin Sultan Al Nahyan.

which followed the visit of his Oil Minister to Libya (supporting the Libyans' nationalisation of BP's assets). The President's decision to exchange diplomatic missions with the Soviet Union is also extremely worrying. We believe that he may have had second thoughts about this in the light of the reactions of neighbouring states and of our own to reconsider. However, it now appears that the decision will stand and that the Soviet diplomats may arrive in the UAE in the near future.

He also added under the heading of Possibility of Replacing Shaikh Zayed:

Thus, we fully sympathise with the Iranians' anxiety about the behaviour and policies of the UAE President. Nevertheless, we are convinced that there is no alternative to accepting that Shaikh Zaid[5] should continue as President for his allotted term (five years). We see great dangers in attempting to replace him, for the following reason:

(a) Zaid is immensely popular within his own state. His great generosity with the Abu Dhabi tribes has earned him their support and respect. Any attempt to replace him with another member of the family would almost certainly precipitate a damaging feud between the supporters of the two rival factions.

(b) [6]

---

[5] This is the spelling of Zayed as it appeared in the original document.
[6] The text of this point is still classified under Section 5 (1) of the Public Records Act in effect from 1958 till 2013.

(c) The machinery of government both of Abu Dhabi and of the UAE is totally dominated by expatriate advisers, most of them Palestinians, Egyptian, Lebanese or Sudanese. These are well entrenched. Their removal would cause the machinery of government to grind to a complete halt as well as precipitating a crisis in the UAE's relations with the more extreme Arab nationalist governments. Thus, any new Ruler would be just as a much prisoner of his advisers as is Shaikh Zaid now.

(d) There can be no question of attempting to transfer the Presidency of the UAE from Abu Dhabi to Dubai. Without Abu Dhabi's money the Federation would collapse. Compared with Zaid, Shaikh Rashid commands very little popular support among the Bedouin. We have little doubt that if the Vice-President were to attempt to assume the Presidency (with or without outside support) there would be a very serious clash between Abu Dhabi and Dubai which would lead to the complete collapse of the UAE. The resulting chaos along the Trucial Coast could only work to the disadvantage of Britain and Iran whose aim has always been to promote stability in the Gulf.

Mr Wright concluded: 'For all of the above reasons, we very much hope that the Iranians will not initiate any action aimed at replacing Zayed.'

In the ministerial meeting of 1 June 1972 of the British Foreign Secretary with Mr Khalatbary, Iran's Foreign Minister, the latter stated that 'the Shah personally is very angry at the behaviour of Shaikh Zayed'.

In the report resulting from this meeting, the British Foreign Secretary wrote:

> Perhaps, the first priority for Mr Khalatbary is the problem created by Mr Zayed, President of the United Arab Emirates, in particular, the hostile attitude he has recently displayed towards Iran (in the statements following his visit to the Sudan, Libya and Syria).
>
> It seems from his[7] insinuations that the Shah may have been thinking about ways and means of replacing Shaikh Zayed. On a number of occasions, His Majesty's Ambassador to Tehran hints at the many difficulties such actions may create. However, it seems that the Shah remains unconvinced by our views. Our main aim in this meeting has to be forcefully disabusing Mr Khalatbary of any lurking inclination to remove Zayed by force, because it will only result in the breaking up of the Federation of the United Arab Emirates, without any guarantee that his successor would be willing to – or be capable of – following more moderate policies.

Iranian Trap!

The Shah of Iran seemed determined to explore his own ways despite British advice. In May 1972, the British and some Iranian delegates tried to convince me to accept an invitation on behalf

---

[7] Referring to Mr Khalatbary's.

of the Shah to visit Iran. Since I was so close to Shaikh Zayed, I always informed him about any invitation. It was revealed later that the Shah's invitation to me to visit Iran was nothing but a trap to attempt to drive a wedge between me and the President, Shaikh Zayed. In a message dated 10 June 1972 by the British Ambassador to Abu Dhabi, C. J. Treadwell, sent to the British Ambassador in Tehran, N. W. Browne, the former wrote under the subheading 'Iran and the State of the United Arab Emirates': 'Thank you for your letter of 26 May, to the Consulate Office, regarding the possible visit of the Ruler of Sharjah to Iran. Such invitation, especially if accepted, may succeed in destroying the relations between Zayed and Sultan.'

Supreme Council Consolidates Power

On Sunday 9 June 1972, a skirmish between Sharjah and al-Fujairah occurred in the area of Kalbaa, and the shooting lasted for two days. Regrettably, four were killed and a small number of people sustained minor injuries. The Federal forces intervened and soon stability and order were restored. This was followed by a meeting held on Tuesday 12 June 1972 in al-Bahr Palace in Abu Dhabi. The meeting had been arranged by HH Shaikh Zayed so that HH Shaikh Muhammad bin Hamad al-Sharqi, Ruler of al-Fujairah, and I could meet, in the presence of HH Shaikh Khalifah bin Zayed Al Nahyan, Crown Prince of Abu Dhabi, HH Shaikh Maktoum bin Rashid al-Maktoum, Prime Minister, and His Excellency Mr Ahmed bin Khalifah al-Suwaidi, Foreign Minister. The dispute between Sharjah and al-Fujairah was discussed with an eye to achieving a lasting peace settlement. For the second time, the Federal authorities had intervened to confirm their ability to deal with internal disputes.

Two weeks after the unfortunate incident, and after seven months of the establishment of the Federation, a meeting of the Federation's Supreme Council on 17 July 1972 was called for, chaired by HH Shaikh Zayed bin Sultan Al Nahyan, President of the State, who was pushing to achieve his goals of establishing a strong State providing security, work, education, medical treatment and housing for all.

In this meeting, the Sharjah–al-Fujairah dispute was brought up, together with the general policy of the State in all fields. The accomplishments realised in the short period of time since the establishment of the United Arab Emirates were pointed out, with particular reference to the provision of basic services to the citizens.

That day, the Supreme Council issued decrees and laws that had the interests of the citizens at heart, among which were:

- Federal Law No. 9 of 1972, concerning Private Schools, governing the rules and regulations relating to the establishment of private schools and placing them under the supervision of the Ministry of Education;
- Federal Law No. 10 of 1972, concerning Educational Missions and the systemisation of the rules and regulations governing the sending of Emirati nationals to study abroad at the expense of the State;
- Federal Law No. 11 of 1972, concerning Compulsory Education. This law made it mandatory for all Emirati

nationals to attend elementary school, and made free all educational stages, be they elementary, secondary or high. This was based on the belief that education is a fundamental requirement for the progress and prosperity of any society;

- Federal Law No. 12 of 1972, concerning the organisation of clubs and associations working in the field of Youth Welfare; and

- Federal Law No. 13 of 1972, concerning social benefits and the systemisation of the rules and regulations governing the payment of such benefits to those who are eligible. This was to provide social care to Emirati nationals and establish the principle of social solidarity.

Discovery of Oil in Sharjah

Buttes Gas & Oil, which had the concession to explore around the island of Abu Musa, managed to dig the first oilfield excavated in Sharjah, which I named '*Mubarak*' (blessed). On Monday 9 October 1972, Sharjah Radio announced the discovery of oil in Sharjah by Buttes Gas & Oil.

I made a speech that day and commended the people of Sharjah for their honourable efforts that had, that day, come to fruition, and I called for greater unity and solidarity to preserve this blessing granted to us by Allah; and so that it might become a shield protecting our federation in its march of progress and prosperity under the leadership of HH Shaikh Zayed bin Sultan Al Nahyan, President of the United Arab Emirates.

After the broadcast of the speech, I headed for the mosque and offered a prayer of thankfulness to Allah, the Almighty. After the *Taraweeh* prayers that evening, I received many groups of well-wishers who came to the General Council to offer their congratulations.

British Ambassador to the United Arab Emirates

The British Ambassador was the same man who had served as the British Political Agent in Abu Dhabi before the establishment of the Federation. This was Charles James Treadwell. During the British military rule of Sudan, he was a judge in Kasala, from 1945 till 1955. Then he became Political Agent in Abu Dhabi from 1968 to 1971. Some of his many colleagues were, for instance, the British Political Agent in Dubai, H. Glen Balfour Paul, who had made the arrangements for deposing Shaikh Saqr bin Sultan al-Qasimi as Ruler of Sharjah on 24 June 1962. There was also their chief, Sir William Luce, who had served in various positions including the following:

- Adviser to the British General Ruler of the Sudan, 1930–56;
- Ruler of Aden, 1956–60;
- Political Resident in the Gulf (known as the President of the Gulf) 1961–6; and
- British Special Representative for Gulf Affairs, 1966–72.
- He also made the arrangements between Britain and Iran regarding the issue of the islands in the Gulf.

It seemed, however, that Mr Treadwell had forgotten his office as Ambassador, and had started fulfilling his personal desire of sending his orders to the Rulers in order to implement his policies. This he did through the British officers who served in the Sharjah Security Directorate, such as Bob Burns and David Nield.

I discussed this issue with HH Shaikh Zayed bin Sultan Al Nahyan, and decided to get rid of them gradually.

This British Ambassador's actions reminded me of the story of the Turkish officer who lost his post following Muhammad Ali Pasha's elimination of Turkish agents in Egypt in the first half of the nineteenth century. The Turkish officer put down a number of pottery jars full of drinking water for people to drink from, as was customary in Egypt at the time. He coloured the jars (*Sabeel* in Arabic) and made them available for everyone's use. However, when a thirsty person came to drink from the red jar, he would shout at him: '*Kharsis* [thief, in Turkish]! Why are you drinking from the red jar?'

'This is a *Sabeel*, isn't it?' the thirsty person would respond.

'No, this is no *Sabeel. Sabeel* is the green jar,' the officer would say. And if a thirsty passer-by took the green jar, the officer would shout, '*Kharsis*! Why are you drinking from the green jar?'

'This is a *Sabeel*, isn't it?' the thirsty person would respond.

'No, this is no *Sabeel. Sabeel* is the red jar,' the officer would say. And, by continuing in like fashion, he satisfied his lust for power and issuing orders.

2

Between the USA and Egypt

FROM 1973 ON, THE EMIRATES as well as Sharjah witnessed a serious of important occasions and events. At a personal level it started with my marriage, when at the end of January 1973 I married Mouza bint Salem al-Mani', who was a relative of my mother. The marriage ceremonies were simple with no big reception or extravagance. We had two children together: a daughter, Azza, and my late son, Muhammad.

At political, social and governance levels occasions and events took place one after another, reflecting our efforts and vision to consolidate the Federation.

Further Leadership of the Supreme Council

The real steps towards consolidating the Federation, along with policies of implementation, were pioneered by the Federation's Supreme Council. On Wednesday 25 April 1973, the Supreme Council held morning and evening sessions, which were followed the next day by a third session. The focus of the meetings was to investigate issues relating to the provision of further services to the citizens of the Emirates, as well as to approve those Federal laws and decrees that would finalise the establishment and consolidation of the State's Federal agencies and institutions.

The Supreme Council also looked into the report prepared by the Prime Minister, HH Shaikh Maktoum bin Rashid, in which the achievements of the Federal ministries in all fields were listed. The report included the following:

Education: The report stated that 30,000 students were receiving education in state schools, and that the aim of the general plan for education was to cater for 50,000 students within three years.

Health: The report highlighted the attention paid to preventive medicine, the provision of health services and the establishment of medical centres in all areas.

Housing: The State was constructing modern houses in Bedouin areas for urbanisation and development purposes. A survey was also being conducted in Umm al-Quwain and in the Bedouin areas in Ras al-Khaimah, in addition to other areas designated for the construction of public housing. The report addressed the efforts made by the State to construct new roads, both internal and external; in particular the Dhaid–al-Fujairah road with a cost of AED 45 million.

Electricity and Water Sectors: New electricity-generating plants were being installed in addition to the extension of new electricity networks. There was also a plan to construct a central 7000-watt plant to link the entire eastern region into one grid. As regards the provision of water services, a survey was being conducted to locate new water sources, to dig new wells, to build water towers in both coastal and internal areas, to improve the utilisation of under-ground water and install modern equipment and pumps.

Agriculture and Fish Resources: It was reported that the State was providing farmers with loans, and helping with the provision of agricultural machinery, the maintenance of farming equipment and the digging of new wells.

Transport: A detailed survey was being conducted regarding the post, telegraph and telephonic services as well as the feasibility of expanding post office services available at that time.

Youth and Sport: The Ministry of Youth and Sport was in charge of the relevant youth activities and had already given away AED 1,000,000 in aid to sport clubs. Scout teams were also being formed and the Ministry was heavily involved in organising Scout camps and jamborees.

Media: The relevant ministry had prepared a Publication Bill, had opened publicity information offices all over the Emirates and had converted *al-Ittihād* to a daily newspaper to become the first daily in the State.

Internal Security: Designated points of entry into and out of the country had been established, coastguard stations founded, and patrols had been conducted at sea. As well, a Federal Police Force had been formed, and a Federal Police College founded.

Defence: A Federal Defence Force had been founded for the purpose of protecting the Federation and preserving the integrity and safety of State territories.

Foreign Affairs: A foreign policy characterised by flexibility towards all the countries of the world was in place based on the State's belief in peaceful coexistence with all peoples of the world.

UAE's Rising Status, and the 1973 War with Israel

Also in this year, 1973, there were a number of occasions on which I strived to make great significance in relation to the emerging standing of the UAE on the regional and international stage. These included regional and international state visits and the UAE position towards the 1973 war with Israel that involved imposing oil embargoes on those countries that supported Israel. I start with four state visits, moving to talk about the war, and ending with another important meeting of the Federation's Supreme Council.

The four visits chronicled here are those of Sultan Qaboos of Oman's visit to the UAE, and my own visits to the United States, the UK and Egypt. The significance of the first one lies in the fact that it came from an important neighbouring state which had had a historical presence and power in the Arabian Gulf for centuries. This visit represented a regional acknowledgement of the Federation and emphasis on the new reality of the Federation. My own visit to the USA and the reception that I received came in the same line of asserting the position of the UAE but at international level and involved a superpower whose influence and presence had replaced that of the British in the Gulf.

On Monday 26 March 1973, a helicopter carrying HH Shaikh Zayed bin Sultan Al Nahyan and his guest, His Majesty Sultan Qaboos bin Sa'id of Oman, landed at the Diyafa Palace in Jumeira (Dubai), where they were received by Shaikh Rashid bin Sa'id al-Maktoum and the rest of the Rulers, the members of the Supreme Council, the Crown Princes, the Shaikhs and the ministers.

A long meeting behind closed doors with Sultan Qaboos was held in the Meeting Hall in the Jumeira Diyafa Palace. Present were HH Shaikh Zayed bin Sultan Al Nahyan, Their Highnesses the Rulers and Crown Princes. Shaikh Kalifah bin Zayed, Crown Prince of Abu Dhabi, had come to Dubai to participate in welcoming Sultan Qaboos bin Sa'id and attended part of the meeting. The relations between the UAE and Oman, and how they could be consolidated, were the topic of discussion.

Sultan Qaboos also visited the *Mirqab* Camp, the headquarters of the Federal forces. During his visit he was accompanied by HH Shaikh Zayed bin Sultan and HH Shaikh Rashid bin Sa'id; and at the camp they were received by HH Shaikh Muhammad bin Rashid al-Maktoum, the Minister of Defence.

The next important state visit was to the USA. After the discovery of oil around Abu Musa Island and once the first well in the newly discovered field had become operational, Buttes Gas & Oil invited me to visit the States. I accepted.

I travelled to the States on Saturday 9 June 1973. My accompanying delegation included: the Head of the National Guard, Shaikh Abdul-Aziz bin Muhammad al-Qasimi; the Vice-President of the Helal Oil Company of Sharjah; the Director of Sharjah Administrative Affairs, Mr Abdul-Aziz Hassan al-Midfa'; and the military escort, Major Ali bin Abdullah al-Muhayyan.

After spending Sunday 10 June in London, we left for Washington, DC, on the morning of the following day, and arrived at Dulles International Airport in Washington just before 3.00 p.m. the same day.

Arrangements with the Ministry of State had already been made through Mr Quincey Lumsden, who was the US Foreign Service Officer for Arabian Peninsula Affairs. However, prior to our arrival, Mr Lumsden had been taken ill and was hospitalised. He was replaced by the Director of Arabian Peninsula Affairs at the Department of State, Mr François Dickman, who later on became the second US Ambassador to the UAE.

I had never met Mr Quincey Lumsden till after he was appointed US Ambassador to the UAE. He was the fourth ambassador, and a friendship between him and me, and between my wife and his, was established that lasts to this day.

On Monday 11 June 1973, immediately after our arrival in Washington, Mr James Akins from the State Department visited me at my place of residence. Mr Akins later on became the US Ambassador to the Kingdom of Saudi Arabia, from September 1973 to February 1976. A friendship between us was formed during his term of office in Saudi Arabia and continued afterwards. He was a supporter of Arab causes and founded an organisation, called 'If Americans Knew', that was a staunch advocate of Arab causes. This organisation was in opposition to the American Israeli Public Affairs Committee (AIPAC), which is both anti-Palestinian and anti-Arab.

The next morning, Tuesday 12 June 1973, I visited the State Department and met Mr Alfred Atherton, Deputy Assistant Secretary of State for the Bureau of Near Eastern and South Asian Affairs. He became the US Ambassador to Egypt from 1979 to 1983. He was also a member of the US negotiating team at the Camp David negotiations which resulted in a peace treaty between Egypt and Israel in 1979; and I saw him on the reviewing stand near President Sadat of Egypt at the time of the latter's assassination.

At 11.00 a.m. that day, I met Hal Saunders who was liaising between the White House and the State Department Bureau for Near Eastern Affairs. Later on, he worked with Henry Kissinger on the drafting of the Camp David Accords.

While we were at the State Department, Mr Rodger Davies invited us to lunch with him. He was appointed US Ambassador to Cyprus in 1974 where, during the demonstrations outside the US Embassy in Cyprus, he was assassinated by a sniper.

On Wednesday 13 June 1973, the Deputy Secretary of State, Mr Kenneth Rush, requested to meet me at the State Department. We met at 4.00 p.m. and my views in the meeting focused on the Arab cause, how to benefit from friendship with the Arabs and how to adopt a neutral position that was not biased in favour of their enemies.

In the evening of Tuesday 12 June 1973, HH Shaikh Salem Sabah al-Salem, the Kuwaiti ambassador to Washington, invited me to a dinner banquet, which was attended by many Arab and non-Arab ambassadors and American officials.

On Wednesday morning, 13 June 1973, we had a tour of the White House in the section that is open to visitors after its residents and staff had left. It was very plain with nothing interesting there to see. At 11.00 a.m., His Excellency Mr Abdullah Saleh al-Maniʿ, Ambassador of Qatar to the US, visited me at my place of residence.

On the same day, I received an invitation to a lunch banquet at the home of the Iranian Ambassador to the US, Mr Ardeshir Zahedi. The house was beautiful and decorated with lavish carpets and exquisite paintings, and it was clear that a fortune had been spent on making it look the way it did. This was no surprise considering that he was married to Ashraf, the sister of the Shah of Iran, and was, therefore, brother-in-law to the Shah.

The Iranian Ambassador took me on a tour of his house while the other guests were drinking their tea. During my visit there, a shameful matter came to light as he invited me to see his chambers. These so-called chambers consisted of a round room with a high dome-shaped ceiling. The walls and the dome were heavily adorned with Islamic carvings. For a while, I thought that this was where he worshipped. However, I was soon disappointed when he started showing me a collection of his drinking glasses. 'The first set of glasses,' he announced, and showed me a glass. Painted on it there was a woman dressed in traditional Iranian garments, her face revealed. He added, 'In these glasses, we start our alcohol drinking session. Then we move to the second set.'

As he said that he showed me a glass from the second set. It had a picture of a woman dressed in traditional Iranian garments, but with her breasts uncovered. 'We move to the third set of glasses,' he continued, 'when alcohol starts turning our heads.' At this point he brought out a glass with a picture of a naked woman. Then the Iranian Ambassador said: 'Now, we come to the fourth set, here ...' By the time he turned to look at me, I was already out of the room. I left him with his drinking glasses and departed from his house, whence my car took me to my own place of residence.

In the afternoon of the same day, His Excellency Mr Ibrahim al-Suwwail, Ambassador of Saudi Arabia, came to visit me.

On Wednesday 13 June 1973 I was invited to a welcoming party by Mr Northcutt Ely, where I was due to give a short speech. However, just before I did so, Marika, Mr Ely's elderly wife, who was sitting next to me, asked: 'How can you tell an Arab man, dressed in his Arab gown, by looking at him from the back?'

Before I could answer her, I was called to address the audience. So, after greeting them, I said, 'Just before coming to the podium Mrs Marika Ely asked me, "How can you tell an Arab man, dressed in his Arab gown, by looking at him from the back?" To this I say, "Marika, you cannot tell that someone is an Arab unless you look at his face".'

On the morning of Thursday 14 June, I went on a tour of Washington, DC, and met the members of the US Congress. I was received by California Senator John Tunney, who presented me to forty congressmen at Vandenberg Hall, where I addressed them. Among other things, I said, 'It is a great honour to be in this great place in this great country. I will talk to you about the Arab man. He is truly like anyone else, with no extra hands or legs. He does not have a tail either. He is a human being just like you, with only one difference: his mind is driven by his heart. So, treat him as you do anyone else.' Then I continued talking about the Arab world and its economic potential. After lunch, I bade them goodbye and set off to the airport to fly to New York.

On Friday 15 June, I was interviewed by the *New York Times*. Then we went to the New York Stock Exchange, where I met an Egyptian man called al-Shahawi. He told me about how he got to New York and how he had worked in the stock market since his arrival from Egypt. He said, 'I worked first as a sweeper, a cleaner, a go-for, and then as a small broker until I became a millionaire.' He also insisted that I visit him in his house. In spite of the fact that time was limited, I accepted his invitation and visited him that afternoon. His house was outside New York and it was a veritable palace set in the countryside.

After our visit to the New York Stock Exchange, we went for lunch in Wall Street at the invitation of General Lucius D. Clay, a director of Lehman Brothers. He was a famous man, having been, in 1942, the youngest general in the US army. He was appointed Deputy to Eisenhower, and also Deputy Military Governor of Germany.

As we talked, the General said that he had visited Sharjah when the US forces were there. 'When we requested permission for the troops to land in Sharjah, the Shaikh refused,' he said. 'I do not know if he was your father or your uncle. But the troops landed there anyhow.'

'It was my father. This was in 1944,' I said, then asked, 'Do you remember that you drove the Shaikh in an amphibious vehicle into the sea?'

'I do', he replied.

'Do you remember the little boy who sat between you and the Shaikh?'

'How can I forget him? He vomited all over me, and so I cancelled the rest of the trip.'

'That boy is the same person sitting in front of you now.'

'You?' he exclaimed in astonishment.

'Yes, me.'

'What a small world!' he said.[8]

In the evening of that day, we visited the headquarters of the United Nations, and met the UN Secretary-General at the time, Dr Kurt Waldheim. We were accompanied by His Excellency, Dr Ali bin Muhammad Humaidan, the UAE Ambassador to the UN. He held a dinner banquet in our honour, inviting a number of ambassadors to the UN.

On the morning of Saturday 16 June, we flew to Houston, Texas, and arrived there at 1.00 p.m. Houston was not much different from Sharjah in terms of heat and humidity but it was lush, with tall trees growing everywhere.

That evening, Crescent Oil Co., which was part of Buttes Gas & Oil, held a dinner banquet and invited around four hundred managers of local oil companies, Houston being the headquarters of most of the oil companies in the United States. At the entrance to the banqueting hall, I stood welcoming the guests. To a man, they were tall with broad shoulders and hands as huge as a camel's foot. They shook hands with me as if they were competing to see who could dislocate my shoulder first. Those who took it easy on my hand shook it to the right and left.

---

[8] See al-Qasimi (2011), *My Early Life*, pp. 3–4.

When I got to the podium, I said, 'I am an Arab, a Muslim; and my Lord commanded me in his Holy Qur'an to say "I believe in Allah, His books and His Messengers". We make no distinction between any of His Messengers; and to Him alone we are *muslimoon* [meaning, in English, 'we surrender'].'

At the entrance, I stood again to bid them all farewell, but, this time, not in the same way as I had received them. Instead, I put both hands behind my back and nodded to them as they left. They accepted this, presumably thinking it was the Arab way of saying goodbye.

The next morning, Sunday 17 June, we visited Mr Douglas Marshall, the founder of the American Arabian Horse Breeders Association, on his own horse farm. He showed us the skills of his Arabian horse Murafiq, which he had bought from Al-Zahraa Horse Farm in Egypt. It was the most beautiful horse of its time, and the most beautiful horses he owned were its offspring. I already knew Douglas as he held the concession to excavate for copper in Kalbaa at that time.

After a meeting and lunch with Dr Atef Jamal al-Deen, Director of the Arab-American Chamber of Commerce in Houston, we went to see a baseball game at the Astrodome, which was covered and air-conditioned. During the game, a massive screen showed the score, but also displayed various announcements and advertisements. One of those announcements read: 'We welcome HH Shaikh Sultan bin Muhammad al-Qasimi, Ruler of Sharjah, guest of Buttes Gas & Oil Co., which has recently discovered oil in commercial quantities in his country'.

The announcement was shown on the screen a number of times, so I said to Mr John Boreta, the CEO of Buttes, 'This reminds me of the English anecdote about a miser who wanted to put a one-sentence obituary in a newspaper after the death of a friend of his, saying *Jo pays his respects to Michelle.* The newspaper publisher suggested to him that this might not be enough and he should fill out the line. So the miser said: 'Put *Jo pays his respects to Michelle and repairs radio sets at such and such address.*' I added, 'Isn't it enough that your company's shares have gone up sky-high since we arrived in Houston?'

Boreta replied, 'Tomorrow, we will put in the papers *Today, Buttes' guest leaves Houston.* The day after, we will put *Yesterday, Buttes' guest left,* and the company's share price will continue going up.'

That evening, Buttes and its partners held a dinner banquet for us in the banqueting hall of the hotel in which we were staying. As I was saying goodbye to the managers of the host companies, a young man approached me speaking in a Texan accent which I could not understand. I just kept nodding my head at him.

In the morning of Monday 18 June, our Houston programme officer called me, requesting that I hurry to the hotel lobby. I answered, 'We still have plenty of time before our trip to NASA.'

'This is not about NASA; it is about the press conference you called for last night,' the programme officer said.

'I did?' I asked.

'The hotel lobby and the conference room are full of journalists and news agency reporters,' he advised.

'I am coming down at once,' I responded. I made my way through the crowds with the cameras flashing from all directions and took my place in the conference room. I greeted them, looking at their faces, and they all started bombarding me with questions. So, I said, 'I did not really call for this conference. There has been a misunderstanding. Last night, I met a young man who talked to me as if he was rolling a small potato with his tongue. I nodded – and the result was this conference.' I answered all their questions, though, then hurried to NASA, where we spent a long time looking around.

Afterwards, we headed for the airport, leaving Texas to fly to Tucson, Arizona. Again, the nod saved me from further shoulder pains, and another person called for a press conference that I had no idea about.

In the evening of Monday 18 June, we arrived in the city of Tucson whose surroundings closely resembled the Dhaid area in Sharjah, with its palms, pomegranate and henna trees and flat plain extending all the way to the mountains.

After attending the dinner held by the University of Arizona, we returned to the hotel. It was no more than a ground-floor complex of buildings whose walls had been built of mud bricks, exactly like those found in the Dhaid area. My room overlooked a small yard, and from my window and close to it I could see a henna tree that had a branch with flowers on it. It was swaying gently and the delightful, cool breeze bore its delicious perfume to my room as if it was greeting me.

The next morning, we visited the Environmental Research Laboratory Superior Farms, where Dr Carl Hegges received us. I had met him two years earlier in Sharjah when he suggested I come to the College of Agriculture at the University of Arizona to do my graduate studies.[9]

---

[9] See al-Qasimi (2011), *My Early Life*, p. 275.

Dr Hegges took me on a tour of the Research Center and introduced me to the researchers there, asking each one to give me a brief idea of his research. One American researcher among them explained, 'My research is on the *Calotropis procera* tree.' As this species of tree grows in the Emirates, I asked in surprise: 'And where did you get it from?'

'I collected the seeds from the area behind your palace in Sharjah,' he said.

Dr Heges then said, 'If you had listened to me that day, you would have been a researcher here.' It was then that I remembered the day I had asked my late brother, HH Shaikh Khalid bin Muhammad al-Qasimi, Ruler of Sharjah, to let me resign from the Ministry so that I could join the University of Arizona in the United States.

After Tucson, we visited Los Angeles, and our journey came to an end at San Francisco airport whence we flew to London on Wednesday 27 June, 1973.

The London Visit

We arrived in London on 28 June 1973, and someone from the British Foreign Ministry received us at the airport to welcome us on our arrival. We had arranged to meet Lord Balniel, the Minister of State for Defence, and later Minister of State for Foreign and Commonwealth Affairs. He already had my résumé which included the following information:

Shaikh Sultan bin Muhammad al-Qasimi, Ruler of the Emirate of Sharjah:

- *Born in 1939 and received his early education in Sharjah. Worked as a teacher in Sharjah School for Vocational Training. Then spent five years studying Agriculture at Cairo University.*
- *After returning to Sharjah, he worked with his brother, Shaikh Khalid.*
- *In December 1971, he was appointed Minister of Education in the Federal government.*
- *After the assassination of Shaikh Khalid, Shaikh Sultan was unanimously elected by the ruling family to be Ruler of Sharjah.*
- *He is of moderate views on religion and politics, has a non-extremist personality and is considered as a moderate nationalist.*
- *His relationship with the British Embassy is good.*
- *He speaks both Arabic and English well.*

Lord Balniel visited me at my hotel on the morning of Friday 29 June 1973 as planned, despite attempts by the UAE Embassy in London to change the date, since, on that same day, both Ambassador Mahdi al-Tajer and Mr Ahmad al-Ubaidali were away, accompanying Shaikh Khalifah bin Zayed Al Nahyan and Shaikh Muhammad bin Rashid al-Maktoum on a visit to Sandhurst College. Mr Mahdi al-Tajer did not want the meeting with Lord Balniel to take place in his absence.

However, that day, Mr Ahmad al-Ubaidali could not make it to Sandhurst and was able to attend the meeting with Lord Balniel and me. The meeting went well, though I felt most uncomfortable when Lord Balniel asked, 'How is your relationship with Abu

Dhabi?', insinuating that it might not have been good. Mr al-Ubaidali looked very uncomfortable, too.

'If there is anything we could help with, Her Majesty's government is prepared to assist Sharjah,' he continued. He also requested that I informed the UAE Embassy in London if I needed anything as the British government wanted to be of service to me. I responded by talking about the old ties Sharjah had with Britain, about the presence of British forces in Sharjah and about the many British people who were well acquainted with Sharjah. I told him that all of these, in themselves, were a great help to me in dealing with the British without disturbing the embassy. Immediately Mr Ahmad al-Ubaidali said that it would be better if I did what was needed through the Foreign Ministry in Abu Dhabi, and not in the old way. I replied that at that time of year the UAE Embassy was always busy with its visitors.

That afternoon, the MP Mr Peter Tapsell held a lunch banquet for me in London. I informed him that Britain had not been as cooperative as it should have been in its assistance to Sharjah, pointing out that previous direct talks between the two parties had come to a halt and had never been resumed. I told him such direct talks would yield the desirable results faster than when a third party is involved.

Egypt: Meeting Sadat

After spending two days in London, it was decided to go from there to Egypt in response to the official invitation extended to me by President Anwar Sadat of Egypt. The visit was planned to last for five days. So, on the evening of Saturday 30 June 1973, we arrived at Cairo airport, and were received by Dr Muhammad Abdul-Qader Hatim, Deputy Prime Minister, and a number of other Egyptian dignitaries. The head of the reception group was the Minister of Al-Azhar Affairs, Shaikh Abdul-Aziz Eisa.

On Sunday morning, 1 July 1973, Dr Muhammad Abdul-Qader Hatim received us in his office, and a number of Egyptian intellectuals had been invited also to the meeting. Among them were two prominent writers, Tawfiq al-Hakim and Yusif Idris. We discussed cultural development in the rural areas.

The next morning we visited the Faculty of Agriculture at Cairo University to meet the professors who had taught me less than two years earlier.

In the Dean's office, a crowd of Faculty of Agriculture professors were waiting and I shook hands with each of them until I reached Dr Sharaf al-Din, who had been my professor in the Department of Animal Sciences. He used to take attendance at every class, and when he got to me he used to mock my name 'Sultan'. He would say: 'Sultan Muhammad Saqr al-Qasimi. Sultan of what? Why do you not choose a different name for yourself? I do not like your name.' A number of times he read out my name as 'Muhammad Saqr al-Qasimi', but I would not answer. So, he would ask, 'Where is he? Is he absent?' And then I would say 'My name is Sultan ... Sultan ... S u l t a n.'

He used to respond angrily, 'Enough ... so I am advised.'

But that day things were different. My parade had arrived with motorcycle outriders ahead of us, sirens going off and the Guard of Honour clearing the way ahead for me to proceed. I held Dr Sharaf al-Din's hand and said: 'So, do you like my name now?'

'You still remember that?' he asked, jokingly.

On the morning of Tuesday 3 July 1973, I met Dr Muhammad Hafiz Ghanem, Secretary-General of the Central Committee of the Arab Socialist Union, at the Union's headquarters in Cairo. We talked about the great achievements realised under President Nasser. That evening, Mr Mahmoud Riyadh, Secretary-General of the League of Arab States, visited me at my place of residence. The following morning, I paid a visit to the Grand Imam of al-Azhar, Shaikh Dr Abdul-Halim Mahmoud, in the Azhar library. I also made a donation for the building of the al-Nour Mosque in Cairo, a project under the supervision of the Grand Shaikh himself. In the evening of that day, I met Anwar Sadat, President of the Arab Republic of Egypt.

On Thursday morning, 5 July 1973, we visited Suez, which had all the semblance of a deserted town. We also viewed some of the front-line posts of the Egyptian armed forces. We were accompanied by the Chief of Staff, General al-Shazli. In addition, we looked across to the other side, at the Israeli Bar Lev Line and its fortifications. A meeting was arranged with Egyptian officers and soldiers at which I applauded their high morale, and stated my faith in their victory in the impending war. Afterwards, the Governor of Suez, Mr Muhammad Badawi al-Khuli, took us on a tour of Suez to inspect the destruction caused by Israeli aggression.

Waiting at the Governor's office, there was a big crowd of the people who had remained in Suez. Among them was Shaikh Hafiz Salama who was trying, with his small entourage, to make his way through to the Governor's office to greet me. When I saw him, I went out and shook hands with him since I knew

41

him from the time he had visited me in Sharjah with a friend of mine, Shaikh Jasim bin Darwish. That had been a few weeks before, when they were collecting donations for the building of the al-Nour Mosque in Cairo.

The war broke out three months later, on 6 October, and, despite initial Egyptian victory, Suez was besieged by the Israeli troops who had managed to penetrate Egypt through the Defrswar enclave. Shaikh Hafiz Salama became a symbol of bravery and resistance. The Israeli troops demanded that the Governor of Suez, Mr Muhammad Badawi al-Khuli, surrender Suez to them.

After consultations with Cairo, it was agreed to surrender. The entrance to Suez was a single road leading to the Arba'een district. The buildings on either side of the road were deserted. However, when Israeli tanks pushed forward into this road, the first and last tanks in the line were bombarded with rockets and grenades. The result was the total destruction of the entire line of tanks, an operation led by Shaikh Hafiz Salama. In her memoirs, Golda Meir, then Israeli Prime Minister, recalled, 'My soldiers cried in fear, *O, mother! O, mother!*'

A Case of Misunderstanding

It was not very long before it became apparent that the visit to my residence in Cairo on Tuesday 3 July 1973 by Mr Mahmoud Riyadh, Secretary-General of the League of Arab States, had afterwards caused a huge disturbance. After our meeting, Mr Mahmoud Riyadh met both Mr Khalatbary, Foreign Minister of Iran, and President Anwar Sadat. As a result, Mr Khalatbary paid Mr Mahmoud Riyadh a visit at his offices at the League of Arab States and informed him that Iran had no plans for territorial expansion in the Gulf region.

Mr Khalatbary also told the British Foreign Office that he had learned from the League of Arab States that I, Shaikh Sultan of Sharjah, had recently brought up the issue of the islands and the revenues from the oil pumped from the territorial waters around them.

The British were disturbed by this news as they were not sure what would become of the agreement made between Sharjah and Iran. This situation persisted without anyone attempting to ascertain from me the veracity of the information.

Then, when His Excellency Mr Afshar, Ambassador of Iran to London, came to visit me, he asked me about what Mr Mahmoud Riyadh had told the Iranian Foreign Minister. I denied the story that had been circulated and stated the truth of the matter: that Mr Mahmoud Riyadh had visited me in Cairo and had informed me that certain Arab states had been working on raising the issue of the islands in a more aggressive way. He proposed an agreement in which the Arab world would give up both of the Tunb Islands (in the eastern Persian Gulf) to Iran in return for Iran's recognition of Arabian authority and sovereignty over Abu Musa Island. On 26 October 1973, after meeting with Mr Afshar, Iran's Ambassador to London, His Excellency Sir Anthony Parsons, Under Secretary of the Foreign Office, wrote to Patrick Wright, Head of the Middle East Department in the Foreign and Commonwealth Office, the following: 'His Excellency, the Ambassador of Iran, seemed convinced and content with this explanation. He agreed with me that this was typically Arab. I told him that we would stop our local agents in the Gulf, and he agreed we should do so.'

Later on it was revealed that Mr Khalatbary had issued his report because the Iranians had been communicating a distorted and untrue version of the story. They had misunderstood what had transpired. Anthony Parsons added in his message to Mr Wright: 'Mr Afshar stated that he thought this was a trait shared by all Arabs. This kind of confusion proves to me that both Arabs and Iranians alike persistently misunderstand things.'

Arab Oil Is Not More Precious than Arab Blood

I returned from Cairo on 7 July 1973. Immediately afterwards, arrangements were made for the Supreme Council of the Federation to convene.

The meeting was held on Saturday 21 July 1973, in al-Manhal Palace in Abu Dhabi. The Prime Minister, HH Shaikh Maktoum bin Rashid al-Maktoum, had provided an earlier report detailing the achievements of the government. The report outlined the difficulties encountered by ministers in terms of carrying out their duties properly. This was an issue for the Supreme Council to discuss. However, the meeting was interrupted and consequently postponed following the news of a hijacked Japanese aeroplane which had landed at Dubai airport. HH President Shaikh Zayed bin Sultan Al Nahyan, HH Vice-President Shaikh Rashid bin Sa'id al-Maktoum and HH Prime Minister Shaikh Maktoum bin Rashid al-Maktoum headed for the airport to examine the situation personally, which was being monitored by HH Minister of Defence, Shaikh Muhammad bin Rashid al-Maktoum.

44

The plane spent seventy hours at Dubai airport, and, after the hijackers had released two Japanese hostages – a man and a woman – the aircraft, with 140 passengers of different nationalities on board, took off again. It flew over Qatar, Bahrain and Basra, then returned to Kuwait, and from there it went to Baghdad before heading for Syria, where it landed at Damascus airport. After refuelling, the plane took off again, but this time for Benghazi, Libya, where it blew up as soon as it landed. Terrified passengers in the airport were scattering in all directions.

On Sunday 22 July 1973, the Supreme Council resumed its session in al-Manhal Palace. The meeting resulted in the formation of a committee under my presidency to further develop the strength of our united entity.

A few months later, in October of the same year, the Arab world was overwhelmed with joy as a result of the victory of the Egyptian armed forces and their success in crossing the Bar Lev Line in the war with Israel. With the increase of hostilities on the war front, HH President Shaikh Zayed bin Sultan Al Nahyan made announcements that drove the entire Arab world even more ecstatic with joy. On Thursday 18 October 1973, HH Shaikh Zayed instituted an oil embargo against those countries supporting Israel. Two days later, Saudi Arabia also announced an oil embargo, on the orders of King Faisal bin 'Abdul-'Aziz al-Su'ud.

These events and the decisions to carry out the embargo prompted the famous statement delivered by HH Shaikh Zayed bin Sultan Al Nahyan during his press conference on 11 November 1973: 'Arab oil is not more precious than Arab blood'.

3

Sharjah Becomes an Oil Exporter

AMONG THE MANY DEVELOPMENTS THAT had speeded the shaping of the UAE and Sharjah in the year 1974, I will focus on four major events: the beginning of oil exportation from Sharjah; Shaikh Zayed's visit to Sharjah and the rest of the country; solving the dispute between Sharjah and Umm al-Quwain; and my own visit to Iran.

Views on America

The 1973 oil embargo imposed by Arab producing countries, discussed in the previous chapter, had a great impact on the West and compounded their concerns about the future of oil supply. Against this background I was interviewed by the *New York Times* in May 1974 about the future of the oil production and exportation from Sharjah. In the interview, I stated that production would begin in a few months. This, I said, would contribute to the hoped-for development of Sharjah as well as the whole of the Emirates. In response to a question about the quantity of oil intended for production, I said that we hoped to pump 80,000 barrels a day that year. I added that sources of revenue other than oil – namely, import taxes and local oil production – had helped to provide the Sharjah Treasury with $12,000,000 in 1973, all of which had been spent on public projects. As for expected revenues for 1975, I said that it was hard to predict revenues since income would depend on world market prices as well as on supply and demand, which were in a constant state of change.

The *New York Times* reporter then asked whether the huge oil revenues might have a negative impact on the hard work and commitment of the Emirati nationals. I said:

> I expect the absolute opposite. There is ample proof to substantiate this. Our people are hardworking and devout and they will not spare any effort in assisting the country to develop and catch up with world advancement. There are many educated Emiratis who have obtained higher degrees, and who work within the government sector and/or hold public offices. They have all proved to be up to the responsibility assigned to them and continue to meet the State's expectations. Their high salaries have not driven them to become complacent.
>
> This success has been a motivating factor in the search by many nationals to improve their social status through learning and by raising their educational and intellectual capacity to join the work force in accordance with their qualifications.
>
> On the other hand, we have devoted special attention to another major sector involving Emirati nationals, that is, the

farmers and owners of private projects. We have offered them technical and financial support, and, additionally to farmers, agricultural equipment. This assistance goes towards helping them in terms of work, production and problem-solving to compensate for lack of experience and to raise productivity.

The American reporter said that he hoped, as an American citizen, that friendship between the Arab States and the US would be established, and asked if that was possible.

I commented:

I have said before that the door of friendship with America stands wide open. Before visiting the US, many people would imagine that the American people were no more than a bunch of murderers, serial killers and cowboys. When I went there myself, I saw a picture totally different from what movies and fictional works depict. I immediately corrected my mindset and the information I had about the American people.

By the same token, you have the wrong idea about Arabs. Zionism has taken total control over your thinking in regard to us. So, if Arab friendship is what you are truly seeking, you have to change your preconceived ideas about the Arabs and how you view them, and try to understand their position and problems. When we can see America well disposed towards us as Arabs, you will, as I have said, find us extending both our arms to warmly shake hands with you as Americans. I have said to a number of Americans before now that you are all paying taxes so that Israel might purchase weapons to kill our children. When we see this state of affairs changing and we see you offering us your hand in peace, you will see us changing in the same direction, too.

Commenting on a question about the future of American-Arab relations, especially after the withdrawal of Israel from Arab territories, I said,

> We are willing to be friends with America as there is nothing we hold against the US and its people, provided that the US ends its alliance with our enemies, and the hand it extends to us is peaceful and blood-free. We also have nothing against Judaism as a religion. It is you in America who confuse Judaism with Zionism. We do not fight, nor do we have any disputes, with Judaism. Our main struggle at present is against Zionism as an imperialistic and fascist system. We are fighting the Zionism that is killing our children, women and young people, as its supporters heartlessly did in the massacre of Deir Yassin. We are an Arab nation where Muslims, Christians and Jews live together. We believe in Allah, His Books and His Messengers. Everyone who thinks that we are against Judaism is wrong, and should know that we are a nation of peace and love, not of aggression and occupation. At the same time, we do not approve of any atheistic beliefs that are contrary to our Islamic faith.

I also commented on manpower issues in agricultural production, saying that the Bedouins comprise a vital sector in the Emirati economy as far as agriculture is concerned. I added: 'Necessary plans are already in place to relocate them to a number of villages around fertile land suitable for agriculture. We are providing them with the required experts and much-needed equipment in order to create a new generation of farmers who are knowledgeable and experienced enough to meet the requirements of the coming stages of development.'

The reporter then asked about my willingness to accept expatriate expertise. I said that all sincere input and expertise that would help us to build our country would be welcome. I averred that the importance of expertise in itself could not be denied, so long as the ultimate aim was to achieve growth, advancement and productive cooperation between the peoples of the world.

I also responded to a question regarding the governance of Sharjah, saying,

We live and work among people of different kinds. We and they are one and the same thing, one family. We accept discussion and sincere dialogue. And we all have patience, so we together sow the seeds and wait till the fruit ripens. We are all in agreement, and look at the future with hope and solidarity. The plan now is to put the right persons in the right place, divide the workload according to specialization and appoint heads who are not only suitable for administering the matters at hand but who will also be at the service of the people. Every person in charge has all the powers for decision-making except in those few cases where a decision is difficult to make. It is then that they will seek the required consultation and necessary advice.

53

Shaikh Zayed's Visit to Sharjah

During his tour in 1974 to bring further unity and together-ness among the Emirates, HH President Shaikh Zayed bin Sultan Al Nahyan visited Sharjah on Monday 13 May, arriving by helicopter at the al-Qasimiyya base at 9.00 a.m. I was at his reception together with a number of officials and Sharjah locals.

HH Shaikh Zayed was accompanied by HH Shaikh Sultan bin Zayed, His Excellency Mubarak bin Muhammad, Minister of the Interior, His Excellency Hammouda bin Ali, Minister of the State, and His Excellency Thani bin Abdullah, Speaker of the Federal National Council.

I accompanied Shaikh Zayed in a car to visit the construction site for the Industrial School, then to Maysaloon School, where a huge reception had been prepared. The school headmistress, Ms Nourah bint Abdul-Rahman Al-Midfi', delivered a speech welcoming HH Shaikh Zayed.

After a tour through the streets of Sharjah, which were adorned with the Federation flags, the President's pictures and posters, the procession made its way to the Sharjah General Council where Shaikh Zayed received Sharjah dignitaries and lunch was served in his honour.

Afterwards, I accompanied HH Shaikh Zayed to the new palace in the al-Ramla district where he could rest. I had already finished the building and furnishing of the palace, but had not moved into it myself at that time.

When we got there, His Excellency Ahmed bin Khalifah al-Suwaidi, the Foreign Minister, was there already. With him was

A meeting of the UAE Supreme Council, on the occasion of the accession of the Ras al-Khaimah Emirate to the Federation in February 1972.

His Highness Shaikh Zayed bin Sultan Al Nahyan tours the Dhaid district of the Sharjah Emirate on Friday 14 April 1972.

His Highness Shaikh Sultan bin Muhammad al-Qasimi donning a medal sash that was bestowed upon him by the Sudanese President Jaafar Nimeiry.

The first flame coming out of the Mubarak oil field marks the beginning of the era of oil production in the emirates, July 1974.

His Highness Shaikh Sultan bin Muhammad al-Qasimi and his Excellency James Akins of the state department, in Washington DC, June 1973.

His Highness Shaikh Sultan bin Muhammad al-Qasimi visits UN Secretary-General Kurt Waldheim in New York, June 1973.

His Highness Shaikh Sultan bin Muhammad al-Qasimi visits the Institute of Environmental Research at the University of Arizona, June 1973.

An exchange between his Highness Shaikh Sultan bin Muhammad al-Qasimi and the Secretary-General of the League of Arab States, Mahmoud Riyadh, July 1973.

His Highness Shaikh Sultan bin Muhammad al-Qasimi in military uniform observes the Israeli Bar Lev line during his visit to the Egyptian front at the city of Suez, July 1973.

His Highness Shaikh Sultan bin Muhammad al-Qasimi addresses Egyptian army officers during a meeting near the frontline with Israel, July 1973.

His Highness Shaikh Sultan bin Muhammad al-Qasimi and His Excellency the Egyptian president Anwar Sadat, July 1973.

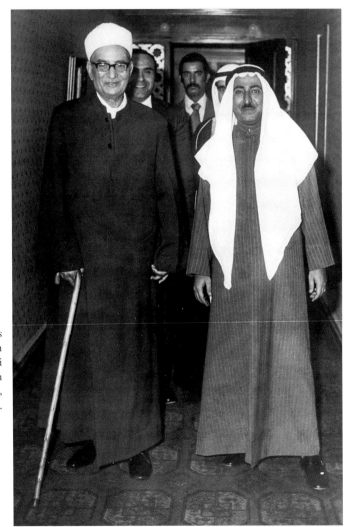

His Highness Shaikh Sultan bin Muhammad al-Qasimi and the Grand Shaikh of al-Azhar in Cairo, July 1973.

His Highness Zayed bin Sultan Al Nahyan visits the Maysaloon School in Sharjah, May 1974.

His Highness Shaikh Sultan bin Muhammad al-Qasimi and the Shah of Iran, May 1974.

Shaikh Sultan bin Muhammad al-Qasimi, the director of the Sharjah oil department and CEO of Buttes, at one of the meetings, July 1974.

His Highness Shaikh Sultan bin Muhammad al-Qasimi inaugurates the production process in the Mubarak oil field, July 1974.

the Prime Minister of Malta, Mr Dom Mintoff, whom Shaikh Zayed received in the new palace. I also attended their meeting.

In the afternoon, HH the President continued his tour of Sharjah, starting with the commissioning of the Sharjah–Dubai highway built by the Ministry of Works. Prior to its reconstruction, this road had been the scene of many traffic accidents. As a result, HH the President had ordered the year before that a parallel road be built so that it became a two-way dual carriageway. Shaikh Zayed cut the ribbon inaugurating the fourteen-kilometre highway that had cost AED 36,377,000 and had taken nine months to complete.

We then went to al-Khaleej al-Arabi Primary Co-ed School in the al-Khan district. The school had twelve classrooms. There we attended a sports and art presentation by the students.

At the end of that day's tour, HH Shaikh Zayed visited the location designated for the construction of public housing in al-Khan. His Excellency Sa'id Hamad Salman, the Minister of Housing, was at this reception. The President signed over the title deeds of a number of citizens, with the rest of the houses being planned for distribution the following month. There were twenty-six public residences that were ready for delivery at that time.

The tour came to an end at 6.30 p.m. when the President headed back to the al-Kharran area in Ras al-Khaimah by helicopter.

Resolving the Dispute with Umm al-Quwain

During his tour to Sharjah, Shaikh Zayed had approached me about the dispute between Sharjah and Umm al-Quwain regarding the oil discovered around the island of Abu Musa. I agreed with him that a percentage of the revenues generated be paid to Umm al-Quwain.

The following day, at noon, just two hours before going to Sharjah airport to fly to Iran for a scheduled visit that I will discuss below, I received a call from Shaikh Zayed requesting that I go to Umm al-Quwain, where he was that day. I obliged and after a discussion involving Shaikh Zayed, Shaikh Ahmad bin Rashid al-Mu'alla, the Ruler of Umm al-Quwain, and myself, it was agreed that Sharjah would pay 30 per cent of its share of the oil discovered in the Mubarak field to Umm al-Quwain.

Also, before I left for my flight, Shaikh Zayed requested that I give 6 per cent of Sharjah's share to the Emirate of 'Ajman, and I agreed to do so.

Zayed and the People's Demands

On Saturday 1 June 1974, less than one month after HH Shaikh Zayed bin Sultan Al Nahyan's tour of the Emirates, he headed a meeting of the Supreme Council of the Federation. Shaikh Zayed had called for this meeting in response to requests from the public, who wanted the government to intervene in the issue of increases in the price of food in the Emirates. All the Rulers attended.

The Council approved that essential commodities, such as rice, sugar and flour, were to be sold to the public, in the first stage, at prices 35 per cent lower than actual cost. AED 28,000,000 was approved in order to provide for the subsidy and to open branches of the National Company for Import throughout the Emirates.

Visit to Iran

From 1972, the British had been trying by diplomatic means to get me to accept an invitation that would be extended to me by the Shah of Iran to visit that country. Every time an attempt was made, I did not reject it but merely excused myself under the pretext that I was too busy and had too many prior engagements.

In early 1974, however, a senior Iranian official visited me and introduced himself as General Nussairi. He said he was carrying an official invitation for me from the Emperor Mohammad Reza Pahlavi, the Shah of Iran. I was not ready to give him an answer at the time, so I told him I would get back to him within a few days. He said he would return then.

In the meantime, I requested to meet Shaikh Zayed bin Sultan Al Nahyan, President of the State, and informed him of the meeting with the Iranian official and the issue of the invitation. Shaikh Zayed approved the visit. So, when General Nussairi returned, I told him that I would accept the Shah's official invitation. We agreed that my visit would be scheduled for 14 May 1974.

On the evening of that date, therefore, I travelled to Tehran for a week-long official visit. Accompanying me on board the private aircraft were the following:

- Shaikh Muhammad bin Sultan al-Qasimi, Head of Petroleum Department;
- Shaikh Hamad bin Majid al-Qasimi, Head of Justice Department;
- Shaikh Abdullah bin Muhammad al-Qasimi, Head of the Emiri Diwan;

- Shaikh Saud bin Sultan al-Qasimi, Head of Sharjah Municipality;
- Shaikh Saud bin Khalid al-Qasimi, Minister Plenipotentiary of the Foreign Office;
- His Excellency Jasim bin Saif al-Midfa', Private Secretary to the Ruler of Sharjah; and
- Major Ali Fahd, the Military Escort.

At Tehran airport, we were very warmly received by General Nussairi, and we were informed that arrangements to meet the Shah had been made for the next day.

On the morning of Wednesday 15 May 1974, I met the Emperor Mohammad Reza Pahlavi, the Shah of Iran, in his palace. He received me standing in the middle of his office and we walked together to our seats while exchanging greetings in Farsi. During our conversation, I quoted some Persian aphorisms and lines of verse by the Persian poets Hafiz and Si'di addressing issues of human nature and the different kinds of people. The Shah was smiling and began to relax in his seat after initially looking tense. He asked about my views on Saddam Hussein's practices towards many people randomly arrested on the streets and dumped at the Iranian borders on the pretext that they were of Persian origin.

I was fully aware of these practices and opposed such acts of barbarism, so I commented, 'What was the fault of the woman who waited in the road for her husband and son who had been kidnapped? What wrong did these people do – people who lost their lives after being dumped at the borders where they were blown up and dismembered by the mines buried there, while, behind them, Saddam's soldiers impelled them towards their slaughter, threatening them with machine guns?'

The Shah interrupted, saying, 'Saddam refuses to accept the agreement signed between us.' 'And who mediated to resolve this issue between us?' he continued. 'Algeria! An Arab country that might have sided with him against us. Yet, we accepted the solutions they proposed.' Then he added menacingly, 'We can teach him a lesson he will never forget. But our relations with all other Arab countries, and our appreciation for all Arabs, prevent us from matching his aggression with aggression of our own.' The Shah then asked me about Afghanistan, and Daoud Khan, who had led a military coup there a year earlier.

'I could bring you Daoud Khan by a leash round his neck and hand him over to you,' I said.

'How?' he asked.

'The leash I mean is a road the Iranian government can build from Kabul to the Sea of Oman through Baluchistan in Iran,' I explained. 'You take care of the road, and we will take care of the marketing. Afghani products will find their way to the Gulf region, and so will imports to Afghanistan from Iran and other Gulf countries,' I continued. 'We need to pay attention to them before Moscow opens a road to them, joining Afghanistan to Moscow,' I added.

'On one condition,' the Shah said.

'What?' I asked.

'That Daoud Khan brings back the twelve officers he sent to Moscow to study.'

'Let's follow the example of the Prophet Muhammad, Peace be upon Him.'

'Elaborate.'

I told this story: 'After one of the battles between the Muslims and the Unbelievers, there was a wounded fighter from the ranks of the Unbelievers who begged for a sip of water. A Muslim went over to him, placed his sword on his neck and shouted at him, "Say you bear witness that there is no god but Allah, and that Muhammad is the Messenger of Allah." On seeing this, the Prophet interfered and said to the Muslim, "Give him a drink first."' As the Shah was a good listener, I added, 'Do not worry too much about the twelve officers. They will return from the Soviet Union hating it.'

'Is that possible?' the Shah asked.

As the saying goes, 'ask an expert'! When I was studying in Egypt, there were some students who had previously gone to Moscow to study. They were cursing the place after their return.

When the meeting with the Shah was over, I bade him goodbye, but he insisted on walking me to the door of the car which was to take me to my place of residence.

The next morning, Thursday 16 May 1974, I met Prime Minister Hoveida. I remember telling him, 'An earthquake in Larestan has no effect on this chair [meaning his official post], but one loaf of bread short in the streets of Tehran can topple it.'

General Nussairi came to visit me and said that the Shah was very pleased with our meeting. 'The Shah thanked me for the arrangements I had made for your visit to Iran,' he added. 'I am very pleased, too, and ready to assist in anything that Sharjah may need, as well as anything you personally request.'

'Could you wait a moment?' I asked. 'I will bring you Shaikh Muhammad bin Sultan al-Qasimi, Head of the Petroleum

Department.' Shaikh Muhammad came and brought with him a copy of the agreement signed between Sharjah and Iran, which stated in one of its articles that Sharjah was directly in charge of running all oil operations around Abu Musa Island.

After reviewing the agreement, General Nussairi asked me, 'And what do you require?'

I replied, 'I need a letter from the Shah stating that the running of oil operations around Abu Musa Island is under my direct authority.'

'Could I take this copy of the agreement with me? I shall bring it back to you,' he asked.

'Of course, I do not mind,' I said.

The next day General Nussairi came back with a message from the Shah written in Farsi and addressed to me. It stated that I was directly in charge of running the oil operations. The General also returned the copy of the agreement he had borrowed.

I left Tehran for Sharjah the following day, 20 May 1974. Arrangements had been made for me to meet the Technical Committee in charge of oil production around Abu Musa Island. This committee had been formed as a result of constant, lengthy disputes and meetings between the Iranian Oil Company and the Sharjah Petroleum Department. Representing Sharjah was Mr Yousri al-Duwaik, my personal legal consultant; Mr Ismael Abdul-Wahid represented the Sharjah Petroleum Department; and Petroleum Engineer Khalili represented the Iranian Oil Company.

Khalili always insisted that he had to co-sign all documents together with Mr Ismael. The pair had a heated argument in the meeting held at the Petroleum Department on 22 May 1974. It got so bad that the committee had to move to my palace in order to settle the dispute. Shaikh Muhammad bin Sultan al-Qasimi attended the meeting. I brought with me the Shah's letter, addressed to me in person, and put it on the table in front of me. No one in the committee had any knowledge of this letter, apart from Shaikh Muhammad bin Sultan al-Qasimi, who had just arrived. Still the parties concerned continued arguing and Engineer Khalili started to raise his voice. Shaikh Muhammad bin Sultan al-Qasimi, who was sitting next to me, whispered in my ear: 'Hit him with it *now*.'

And every time Khalili raised his voice, Shaikh Muhammad repeated 'Hit him with it.' Eventually, I had had enough and I showed the letter to Engineer Khalili. As soon as he read it, he kissed it, raised it above his head and then apologised for the way he had been acting.

On the evening of Tuesday 28 May 1974, I met with HH Shaikh Zayed bin Sultan Al Nahyan at the al-Bahr (the Sea) Palace and reported to him what had transpired during my visit to Iran.

One final note about my visit to Iran involves General Nussairi, who organised the trip. A couple of weeks after the visit, in early June 1974, the British Consul in Dubai, Mr A. E. Saunders, visited me to ascertain how the visit had gone. I told him about General Nussairi and the huge number of officials who were at our service during the visit in Iran. Saunders commented, saying, 'You were in the hands of the SAVAK.'

'How?' I asked.

'General Nussairi is the Head of the disreputable Iranian National Intelligence and Security Organisation, known as SAVAK,' he answered.

Exporting Oil from Sharjah

The Crescent Petroleum Co., which had concessionary rights to drill for oil around Abu Musa Island, had already dug three oil-producing wells and were drilling a fourth. Crescent Petroleum was an umbrella name incorporating Buttes Gas & Oil Co. which owned 35 per cent of the shares. Other partners were:

- Ashland Oil Ltd, with 25 per cent;
- Skelly Oil Ltd, with 25 per cent;
- Kerr-Megee Corp Ltd, with 12.5 per cent; and
- Juniper Oil Ltd, with 2.5 per cent.

The managers of all these companies came to Sharjah to participate in the celebrations relating to the start of exportation of oil from Sharjah. They arrived at the Ruler's palace on Wednesday 17 July 1974, where a luncheon banquet had been prepared in their honour and which was attended by Sharjah dignitaries.

On the morning of Thursday 18 July 1974, I inaugurated production operations of the three wells at the Mubarak field with a total capacity of 60,000 barrels per day. After returning to Sharjah, the Sharjah Emiri Diwan issued the following statement informing the public of the good news:

HH Shaikh Sultan bin Muhammad al-Qasimi, Ruler of Sharjah, has announced the commencement of oil exportation from the Mubarak field in the seabed around Abu Musa Island. This follows the announcement by the American consortium headed by Buttes Gas & Oil Co. regarding the completion of all technical preparations for the exportation of the oil.

Buttes has also announced that, in the first month, about 50,000 to 60,000 barrels of oil per day would be exported; however, the production platform constructed to receive the oil is equipped to handle up to 100,000 barrels per day. The capacity of the crude oil reservoir of Birkat al-'Aim, which is only one mile from the production platform, is 640,000 barrels per day. The company's announcement also noted that a final check revealed that the production equipment for the three wells in the Mubarak field had been found to exceed the requirements. The company has also announced that the fourth Mubarak field, one and a half miles from the existing wells, was about to dry out. A test will be conducted in mid-August.

In making this announcement about the state of oil exports the Emiri Diwan asks Allah to grant us more of His blessings and that this would bring prosperity to Sharjah, the Emirates and the entire nation. The government of Sharjah is exerting its utmost efforts, under the leadership of HH the Ruler of Sharjah, to achieve greater prosperity and ensure proper utilisation of Sharjah's natural resources to contribute to the development of the country, raise the people's standard of living and support aspirations for unity and for decent living.

On the afternoon of the same day, Crescent Petroleum held a lunch celebration at the Carlton Hotel in my honour to celebrate the occasion of exporting the first oil shipment from Sharjah. It was attended by a large number of Sharjah officials. I delivered a brief speech in which I said:

> It is indeed a happy occasion today to celebrate the export of oil from the Mubarak field. The operations conducted by the company at an earlier stage are considered to be one of the most remarkable achievements in the oil-mining sector in terms of speed of execution. Therefore, I should like to thank all who contributed towards this great accomplishment.
>
> Now that we are witnessing positive changes in this great country, which aspires to a future filled with opportunities for decent living, wellbeing and peace of mind, we do not intend to allow matters to take a haphazard course; rather, a comprehensive, well-conceptualised plan has been developed to deploy the revenues generated in the most proper of ways. The plan has the citizens as its main focus point in order that we might create a well-balanced and robust society. The first stage of the plan has already begun to manifest itself in terms of creating mega-projects and the like.
>
> I pray to Allah, the Almighty, to grant us success in our endeavours to serve this Emirate and its great citizens, the people of the United Arab Emirates and the Head of the State, HH Shaikh Zayed bin Sultan Al Nahyan.

4

The Hope We Lost

ON TUESDAY 25 MARCH 1975, the Arab world was saddened by the shocking death of King Faisal bin 'Abdul-'Aziz al-Su'ud of the Kingdom of Saudi Arabia. He had been shot by a member of the Saudi royal family and died as a result. Widely popular in the region, King Faisal's greatest wish had always been to perform *salah* (prayer) in the Aqsa Mosque in a Palestine that had been freed from the yoke of Zionist occupation.

One of King Faisal's memorable statements was:

The Kingdom of Saudi Arabia considers itself a dedicated agent of support for every Arab, and puts itself at the service of every Arab. This country aims to achieve cooperation, solidarity and brotherhood among all Arabs. By the same token, the Arab world expects us to commit ourselves to intrinsically Arab causes, to the liberation of all Arab countries, and to have at heart, as our main objective, the interests of Arabs.

The tragic incident took place while King Faisal was going about his official duties. That morning Prince Faisal bin Musa'id bin 'Abdul-'Aziz, a nephew of King Faisal, approached King Faisal on the pretext of greeting him. When he was close enough, he fired a number of shots directly at the King. It was later revealed that the Prince was emotionally unstable and had acted totally on his own. King Faisal was rushed to the hospital where he passed away as a result of his injuries.

The Saudi royal family decided that Crown Prince Khalid bin 'Abdul-'Aziz al-Su'ud should succeed to the throne, and that Prince Fahd bin 'Abdul-'Aziz al-Su'ud be appointed Crown Prince.

His Highness Shaikh Sultan bin Zayed Al Nahyan, President of the State, led the delegation comprised of HH Vice-President Shaikh Rashid bin Sa'id and the Rulers of the Emirates. On 26 November 1975 they all left for the Kingdom of Saudi Arabia to offer their condolences.

I was not part of this delegation as that day I was in France at the end of a visit to that country. The following day I headed for Tunisia on another official visit.

Connecting with Other Countries in 1975

In 1975 I made a number of official visits with various objectives to the following countries: Kuwait, Italy, France, Tunisia and Egypt.

Kuwait

On the morning of Saturday 15 March 1975, I made an official three-day visit to Kuwait in response to an invitation from HH

Shaikh Sabah al-Salem al-Sabah, Emir of Kuwait. We arrived at Kuwait airport just before noon. We were received by:

- Shaikh Jaber al-'Ali, Deputy Prime Minister and Minister of Information;
- Mr Abdul-Aziz Hussain, State Minister for Cabinet Affairs and Head of the Reception Committee delegates;
- Shaikh Nawaf al-Ahmad al-Sabah, Governor of Hawli;
- His Excellency Mr Saif al-Jirwan, Ambassador of the Emirates in Kuwait; and
- a number of other senior officials in Kuwait.

During my visit, I met HH Shaikh Sabah al-Salem al-Sabah. I also met the Emirati students who were then studying at Kuwait University.

Italy
On Tuesday 18 March 1975, I flew from Kuwait to Italy on an official visit. In Rome, I met Mr Mariano Rumor and discussed Italian-Emirati bilateral relations with him. Other meetings were also held with delegates from a number of Italian companies; in particular, we met experts in the field of electricity.

France
On Thursday 20 March 1975, I flew from Rome to France following an invitation from President Valéry Giscard d'Estaing. My visit lasted for a week, during which I met the French President in the Élysée Palace. I presented him with a gold sword on which a line of Arabic poetry was inscribed. He asked me to

translate it for him, but I said, 'If I am to translate this line for you, the time for this meeting would run out. Instead, I have made an English translation of it on this piece of paper.'

He took the paper, then asked, 'What do you think of French politics?'

'It is like this white *thawb* [gown],' I said. I was wearing my Arab gown and I pointed at it. Then I took a pen off the President's desk and put a dot of ink on the robe at chest height. 'But now this *thawb* is no longer the way it used to be,' I added.

'And what is that black dot?' he asked.

'There are people who claim to represent France and they are acting against the unity of Algeria. In the Arab world, we interpret this as France's unwarranted interference in the affairs of Algeria.' I meant to say to the President that French politics was sound and would look as pure as my white gown, except for a tainting dark spot, the dot I had added on my white gown, which represented France's policy towards Algeria. The President then picked up a pen and wrote down my observation.

We talked in detail about the issue of Djibouti, that part of Somalia under French occupation. I proposed that France should be reconciled with the two disputing parties there before its withdrawal, and develop a constitution whereby the two parties could rule jointly.

Then the President's office door opened and an aide-de-camp looked in, whereupon the President made a subtle gesture with his hand, telling him to leave. I realised then that I had already taken up more time than had originally been allotted for my meeting.

While still in France, I had several meetings with French

company directors who offered to contribute to the development of Sharjah.

Tunisia

On Wednesday 26 March 1975, we travelled to Tunisia on an official visit following an invitation from President al-Habib Burqaiba. This invitation had been received through his son, al-Habib Burqaiba, Jr, when he visited me in Sharjah on 2 January 1975.

When I arrived in Tunis, the capital, I stayed at the Republican Palace, in a suite near where al-Habib Burqaiba resided. We met many times during my visit.

On 27 March, I had a meeting with President Burqaiba in the presence of Prime Minister al-Hadi Abu Nuaira, Foreign Minister al-Habib al-Shatti and the Ambassador of the Emirates to Tunisia. The President also held a dinner banquet which was attended by a number of senior Tunisian officials.

The next day, I had a tour of the Zitouna Mosque in the old city, and visited an exhibition of hand-made products. In addition, we went to a number of economic facilities and a variety of libraries, where I saw some of the most famous and important Islamic manuscripts.

The following morning, President Burqaiba received me in his office at the Republican Palace where I was decorated with the Tunisian Insignia in appreciation of the brotherly relations that existed between Tunisia and the Emirates. This was in the presence of Prime Minister al-Hadi Abu Nuaira and Foreign Minister al-Habib al-Shatti. Afterwards, I presented President Burqaiba with a gold dagger. Then we paid a visit to the ancient

Islamic city of Qairawan and to Djerba Island, an attractive tourist resort.

On 30 March, we paid a visit to Monastir, the birthplace of Burqaiba. The next day we left Tunisia for Egypt.

Egypt

We arrived in Cairo on 31 March 1975 on a four-day official visit. We were received at Cairo airport by Prime Minister Dr Abdul-Aziz Hegazy, whom I had met before, having once visited his office in central Cairo when he was Professor of Accounting at Cairo University. At the time, I was still a student in the Faculty of Agriculture at Cairo University.

On this trip in 1975 we were also met by some important ministers, the UAE Ambassador to Egypt, His Excellency Taryam bin Imran bin Taryam, and several Arab ministers.

The Egyptian honour delegation that accompanied us during our visit was headed by Dr Mahmoud Abdul-Akher, Minister of Agriculture, who had been my Professor of Vegetable Crops, and was now Dean of the Faculty of Agriculture. Also present was Mr Ibrahim Sha'rawi, the Cabinet Head of Ceremonies.

On the morning of 1 April 1975, official talks started at Cabinet headquarters. The Egyptian delegation was led by Prime Minister Dr Abdul-Aziz Hegazy. Afterwards, we headed for the People's Assembly (the Egyptian Parliament) to meet the Speaker, Sayyed Mar'i.

The following day, I had a meeting with President Anwar Sadat. We met after the *Maghrib* prayer in a villa in al-Qanater al-Khayriyyah. I was accompanied by the UAE Ambassador to Egypt, His Excellency Taryam bin Imran bin Taryam.

President Sadat received us at the top of the open stairs leading to a room on the second floor of the villa. I shook hands with him, as did the Ambassador. Then the President put his arm behind my back and ushered me up the narrow stairs, step by step. 'Welcome!' he said. 'Welcome to a son of Egypt!'

During the meeting, Sadat talked about the circumstances of the war he had initiated in 1973, and complained that the Soviets had not supplied him with weapons. I interrupted him: 'The late President Jamal Abdel Nasser, may Allah rest his soul, had made all the preparations for that war before his untimely death.' As I said that, Sadat picked up a lighter and lit the pipe he was holding in his hand. He puffed smoke a number of times and then exhaled all at once, making what appeared to be a cloud of smoke behind which he took shelter. As Sadat looked angry,[10] Ambassador Taryam bin Imran bin Taryam interrupted and changed the subject, asking: 'How are your relations with Syria?'

'Good,' the President replied.

This was followed by complete silence, and consequently I felt obliged to leave. So I stood up and extended my hand to say goodbye. The president stretched his hand out from behind the table and said, 'Goodbye.'

On Wednesday 3 April 1975, there was a meeting at the headquarters of the League of Arab States with Mr Mahmoud Riyadh, its Secretary-General. After the meeting, we went to the UAE Embassy in Cairo, where I met the staff of the embassy.

On Thursday 4 April, I met Dr Muhammad Hafiz Ghanem,

---

[10] Sadat was envious of Nasser's legacy and popularity, and wanted to take all the credit for the 1973 victory over Israel. Mentioning Nasser with praise and admiration used to irritate him.

Secretary-General of the Central Committee of the Arab Socialist Union, at the Union's headquarters. Less than two years earlier, I had met Dr Ghanem in his office and he had praised the rule of Abdel Nasser. On this day, I visited him again in the same place. It seemed that nothing had changed except for him. He opened his conversation with me by saying, 'What did we get from the era under Abdel Nasser? He left us with junk factories, and a High Dam that has blocked the flow downstream of alluvium silt which has destroyed Egypt's agriculture.'

I stopped him there: 'Are you saying the factories are junk? Are you talking about the armament factories in which the UAE government has bought shares and paid millions of dollars for? Well, I must take this to the UAE government to get them to disinvest in these overpriced factories that have nothing but a spurious value to them. As for the High Dam, it protects Egypt in times of drought, produces cheap power, with electricity cables reaching even the most remote towns and villages.' I then excused myself, and left him fuming and talking angrily to the reporter Zakaria Neel, who was present before and after my meeting with Dr Ghanem.

Later, Zakaria told me, 'Before your arrival, Dr Ghanem had asked me about Your Highness and I told him you were a son of Egypt. After you left, Dr Ghanem shouted and said, "Is this just a son of Egypt? He knows Egypt more than one born and bred in the heart of Giza, and cannot be bluffed".'

I returned to Sharjah on 6 April 1975.

5

One Nation, One Flag

THE ESTABLISHMENT OF THE FEDERATION of the United Arab Emirates was a new experience in the region, but the passage of time was proving it to be successful in spite of the initial difficulties encountered along the way. The first stage was characterised by the formation and establishment of State institutions. At that point in time we had entered a new phase and were accomplishing major achievements as we began addressing any problems and overcoming obstacles in the path of future progress.

After an intense and detailed five-month study, I had submitted a report to the Federation's Supreme Council meeting on Wednesday 9 January 1974. The ten-page report had been compiled by a committee I had chaired which was commissioned to investigate ways and means of consolidating the Federation. In spite of the fact that the report included many suggestions on how to tackle problems and obstacles in various aspects of different national sectors, and on how to push forward to the next stage of national progress, nothing had been done about the report as a whole or any part thereof.

On 26 April 1975, the Supreme Council convened, chaired by HH Shaikh Zayed bin Sultan Al Nahyan. The Council focused on discussing proposals and measures that would assist in consolidating the Federation and help it achieve its goals. These were all included in a report prepared by a Ministerial Committee headed by the Prime Minister, HH Shaikh Maktoum bin Rashid al-Maktoum.

HH Shaikh Zayed: Frank and Determined

The UAE President, HH Shaikh Zayed bin Sultan Al Nahyan, spoke to the local media on Tuesday 21 October 1975. This was one of the most important and significant press conferences held since the inception of the state of the UAE. During that press conference, Shaikh Zayed dealt with many of the internal issues, summarised below, and proffered his vision regarding the stages of national development to follow. He also dealt with his responsibilities as President – as well as the responsibilities of the members of the Supreme Council and those of ordinary citizens – of impelling the Federation forward towards a new future where all obstacles would be surmounted.

HH Shaikh Zayed also emphasised the fact that the defence forces had guaranteed stability and had established national security. This state of affairs would help in the equitable distribution of responsibility and identify those accountable if anything were to go wrong. Shaikh Zayed said, 'Every Ruler has to ensure the stability of the State, and Rulers should not pursue contradictory goals – for the entire nation looks up to them and expects a lot from them. We have to put aside personal interests for public interest. This is what will unify us and will achieve prosperity and welfare for everyone.'

Addressing the issue of the freedom of expression and the right of criticism, HH Shaikh Zayed said:

> We believe in freedom and preserving the dignity of all citizens. The press is part of this nation; it represents the conscience of the people. Therefore, we have to welcome constructive criticism from the press since we are all partners in opinion-formation, planning and execution. Our objective is to realise everything that is in the public interest and help to build our country.
>
> It is regrettable that contradictions exist in what is being propagated in the State's mass media and this must be rectified.

HH the President also pointed out the importance of coordination between the various Emirates in terms of industrial projects and the like. He said, 'The economy of this nation needs to be an interconnected whole ... and every project established needs to serve the whole of society so that prosperity might be achieved for all.'

In addition, HH Shaikh Zayed talked about the National Federal Council: 'We welcome the views of all the sons and daughters of the Emirates, and we seek always to know their opinions and share responsibility with them on all issues, big or small. We are all soldiers of this country, and those who do not consider themselves to be such are not one of us.'

Administrative corruption was another issue dealt with. HH Shaikh Zayed said, 'The success of this nation will not be possible in the presence of corruption – which is a malignant disease that must be eradicated from our presence. We do not wish to contend with this type of disease in our midst. We must be fully vigilant so as to protect ourselves and our children. Anyone deviating from the right path must be held accountable and shown no tolerance – the public commonwealth must be protected at all times.'

On the State's efforts to alleviate the burden of the high living costs for citizens, and on the subsidy provided by the State through the National Trading Company in terms of selling foodstuff at low, affordable prices, HH Shaikh Zayed said, 'Traders must realise that this company has been established to serve the interests of our people. In consequence, traders' own personal interests have to fade away in favour of what achieves most benefit for the general public.'

In response to a question about the possibility of nationalising the oil industry of the UAE, Shaikh Zayed said, 'The issue of nationalisation is not under consideration at the present time as we are in need of the expertise that can administer this industry efficiently; and we do not yet have the required qualified national cadres to do so. Furthermore, we do not want to replace one set of foreign expertise with yet another foreign one.'

On the possibility of expanding the Federation he stated, 'The door is wide open for our brothers in Qatar and Bahrain to join the State of the UAE. We all have the same interests.'

After the conference, I met with HH Shaikh Zayed in the presence of the Foreign Minister, His Excellency Mr Ahmad bin Khalifa al-Suwaidi. I presented to them the decisions I was planning to implement to strengthen the Federal entity of the UAE that would not only serve as practical steps for the way forward, but that would also serve as exemplars to be followed by all the other rulers. HH Shaikh Zayed approved.

Decisions Consolidating the Federation

I delivered a speech at the inauguration of the new headquarters of the Sharjah Traffic Department on Tuesday 4 November 1975, and attended the celebrations accompanying the event. My speech went as follows:

> In the name of Allah, Most Gracious, Most Merciful. Dear brothers and honourable citizens, I should like to greet and welcome you today, and thank you for attending the inauguration of this new institution – the Sharjah Traffic Department – which is but another step forward towards consolidating our federation.
>
> My brothers, I should like to speak to you today openly, for I believe in the same things that you believe in; and I am keen to achieve the things that you wish for.
>
> Political division is indeed a reality that has been imposed upon us in the Arab world from the Arabian Gulf to the Atlantic Ocean. This has occurred despite the status we had achieved in days of yore of being one nation, having a unified identity, and existing as one entity for many centuries.
>
> There does not seem to be any objective basis today in our Arab world for such political division; indeed, the same applies to all aspects of division that we presently witness as regards our different peoples, countries, cultures and/or interests.
>
> One thing we have learned from history is that dividing the Arab nation has always been a process of hacking one body into many pieces, with a resulting divergence of interests. We see this clearly revealed in the arena of the Arab world.
>
> From here, brothers, on the banks of the Gulf, we keenly

scrutinise what is taking place in the broader Arab homeland because we believe that we share the same destiny; by so doing, we confirm our identity as Arabs, and actualise our nationalism. What has been happening in Lebanon,[11] for example, is but a manifestation of the kind of tear that is ripping asunder the fabric that binds Arab society, and, likewise, a manifestation of a schism that has been wrought upon us, the Arab people. The ongoing disputes and differences of opinion between Arab brothers about the central issue[12] is another illustration of the discord imposed on us Arabs by foreign agencies in order that we remain divided and incapable of rising again as one united, Arab nation.

Dear brothers, we, the Arab people, reject division and abhor disputes. The people of the United Arab Emirates – we, too, reject division and abhor disputes. We believe in unification as our ultimate destiny. We strive towards strengthening our unity as much as we possibly can. We strive resolutely towards the firm establishment of our fledgling state so that it might finally emerge as one unique entity after all these years of constant discord.

For the proper formation of our State and for our nation-building, the current environment requires effort on an unprecedented scale. It requires the rejection of disputation, the abolition of contrariness, the rectification of past errors, and our transcendence above personal conflict and divisive issues. Brothers, we must all ensure the stability of our country and

---

[11] Referring to the then civil war in Lebanon.
[12] Referring to the Palestine issue.

protect our new State so that it might stand up, tall and proud.

Fellow citizens, the people today require their Rulers to merge all local agencies into one united Federal body, under one banner and under one President. And I do not think that anyone among us will think otherwise or will stand against the desires of the people. This resolve of our citizens has its own power, weight and due process. In your name, from this place, I declare that complete integration is indeed an inevitable necessity that is required by the current stage in the development of our State; particularly, that is, after our four years of trial and error, of positives and negatives.

In a few days' time, we will be celebrating the anniversary of the establishment of our State and of our independence. We have to provide our people, who have lived through division and who have witnessed its negative impact, proof positive of our belief, resolve and determination to go forward towards accomplishing the greatest goal of all – that is, of unity, as well as of supporting our President who has sacrificed so much, and has exerted so much effort to improve this country and to impel its great people towards prosperity.

Brothers, in your name, I should like to announce the incorporation of:

1. The Sharjah Police and Public Security Departments into the Federal Ministry of the Interior;
2. Our local Justice Departments into the Federal Ministry of Justice;
3. Sharjah Radio into the Federal Ministry of Information;
4. The Sharjah Department of Cable and Wireless

Communication into the Federal Ministry of Transport; and

5. The National Guard as a security force in Sharjah into the Federal Ministry of the Interior.

The integration of these departments into the Federal entity means that our entire citizenry becomes part of the advance forward of our unified nation, thereby committing ourselves to an all-embracing unity. Here in Sharjah, we proclaim loudly and clearly that this is our objective.

In conclusion, I express my sincerest wishes for the prosperity of the people of the Emirates under the leadership of HH Brother Shaikh Zayed bin Sultan, President of the State. May Allah direct him towards what is right so that he might guide us in our service to our Arab nation, and lead us to the accomplishment of a heroic victory on behalf of the whole of the Arab world.

Thank you.

Immediately after my speech, the flag of the State was raised on the flagstaff over the new Traffic Department building.

On the same day, after I had announced these decisions, a crowd of journalists from the Emirates and other Arab countries gathered for a question and answer session. The press conference lasted for an hour, during which I answered questions that focused mainly on the measures that would need to be taken because of the resolutions adopted. Some significant questions came from the following quarters:

Q: Why are these decisions being made so close to the convening of the Supreme Council of Rulers? [Abdullah al-Nuwais, Abu Dhabi TV]

A: Firstly, these decisions are not new or specific to this particular time. The issues related to them have always been of concern to State officials since the creation of our Federation. We have been trying to support our Federation in every possible way; and, as a result, these resolutions have been taken to put an end to those issues that have revealed themselves as obstacles in the path of our Federation's way forward – obstacles that could impede the progress desired by our people. The resolutions taken are in response to what the people want – that is, merger and unification. Our goal has always been unity – and though we may have not discerned the means to do so initially, we can now rise above difficulties that have evolved to become mere formalities that should not have obstructed our efforts in the first place.

We have taken these initial steps and have announced the merger of local institutions with Federal ministries. This will surely be followed by other steps, *inshallah*, in order that further advances, greater inter-connectedness and firmer solidarity might be realised for the sake of the safety and security of the whole region.

Q: After taking those decisions, what is the first priority that you think should be on the agenda of the Supreme Council when it convenes? [Khalid Muhammad Ahmad, *al-Ittihād* newspaper]

A: What has happened to date has been just the first step forward; and we are not going to stop there – rather, we shall continue our efforts and endeavour towards achieving greater unity and closer cooperation. In the Supreme Council, my efforts as an active member will go beyond what has been accomplished so far. We need to move to the final stage of complete unification and integration in response to the wishes of the people. This is our duty, a duty that we will fulfil, if not today, then tomorrow – because it is a solemn duty that we have been entrusted with. I pray that Allah will guide us in our efforts.

By the end of that day I received a telegram of congratulations from HH Shaikh Zayed bin Sultan Al Nahyan, praising the steps that I had taken.

Not only this but on the evening of the following day, Wednesday 5 November 1975, HH Shaikh Zayed bin Sultan Al Nahyan himself came to Sharjah to congratulate me personally and to join in the celebrations. Crowds gathered in front of the Sharjah Public Council to wait for the arrival of the President who was received with national songs and ballads as well as flags and welcoming placards. While HH Shaikh Zayed was extending his praise and congratulations, a massive crowd of jubilant citizens entered the *majlis* wanting to shake hands with HH and myself and to congratulate us.

Replacing the Flag

On the morning of Thursday 6 November 1975, I was expecting the arrival of a public demonstration in support of the decisions I had made. The march started at sunrise – long before its scheduled time – from the entrance of Sharjah city.

By 10.00 a.m., the demonstration had attracted more than 10,000 participants and it marched its way through the streets of Sharjah to the Public Council buildings. Banners with pictures of HH Shaikh Zayed and myself were flown, in addition to placards in support of my aforementioned decisions and other placards requesting complete unity and the eradication of corruption.

In the midst of the thousands of people – most of whom were employees in either the government or private sectors, but comprised school students as well – I stood on a table placed near the flagpole on which the national flag of Sharjah was flying. I held the flag of the Federation in my hand and addressed the people saying, 'This State has one President and one flag. Let us practise what we preach and replace the Sharjah flag with that of the Federal one. Let it fly over all the institutions and agencies of Sharjah.' And then I replaced the flag while the crowd cheered.

Some citizens felt uneasy about the removal of the Sharjah flag and grumbled, 'Sultan has removed the flag of al-Qawasim'.[13] So, I had to explain to them the true history of that flag.

---

[13] Al-Qawasim refers to my tribe and its broad base which ruled Sharjah for centuries.

This flag is known to the British as the second flag. It is white with red in the middle. Ships coming into or exiting from a port in Britain would hoist it to announce that the ship had a captain on board. After defeating the al-Qawasim tribe, the British occupiers gave the Qawasim this flag to replace their own flag, which used to have three horizontal colours: green, white and red from top to bottom, with a Qur'anic inscription: 'A victory from Allah and an imminent conquest' on the white part. The loss of our original flag took place on Saturday 8 January 1820. So, what I have done now is to restore dignity to the citizens of Sharjah of today and to the citizens of Sharjah of times past, all of whom have been obliged to salute the flag of the very aggressors who had removed our own flag, a flag that had symbolised the struggle of the Qawasim.

Soon after that the flags of other Emirates were lowered and the flag of the Federation was raised. At the meeting of the Supreme Council of 15 November 1975, the Rulers of 'Ajman, Umm al-Quwain and al-Fujairah agreed to follow the steps taken by me and to merge their local institutions and agencies with the relevant Federal institutions, and to replace their own flags with that of the Federation.

The President and Ruler of Abu Dhabi, HH Shaikh Zayed bin Sultan Al Nahyan, then took the decision to replace the flag of Abu Dhabi with that of the Federation. He also decided to contribute 50 per cent of Abu Dhabi's revenues to the general revenues of the UAE, to establish the University of the United Arab Emirates and to bring into being a National Commission for Accountability.

6

Communism in Somalia and
Islam in America

In Somalia

IN RESPONSE TO AN INVITATION by President Siad Barre, I went to Somalia on an official visit on Sunday 18 January 1976. The delegates accompanying me were:

- HH Shaikh Muhammad bin Sultan al-Qasimi, Minister of Works;
- HH Shaikh Abdullah bin Muhammad al-Qasimi, Minister of the Sharjah Emiri Diwan;
- HH Shaikh Saud bin Sultan al-Qasimi, Head of the Sharjah Municipality;
- HH Shaikh Saud bin Khalid al-Qasimi, Foreign Ministry Plenipotentiary;
- His Excellency Taryam bin Imran bin Taryam, UAE Ambassador to Egypt;

- His Excellency Abdullah bin Imran bin Taryam, Minister of Education;
- Mr Jasim bin Saif al-Midfaʻ, Personal Secretary to the Ruler of Sharjah;
- Mr Abdul-Rahman Bukhater, Head of Sharjah National Bank; and
- Major Ali bin Abdullah al-Muhayyan, Personal Escort.

Bidding me goodbye as I left on my visit was a group of senior officials (as well as ordinary citizens) led by the Minister of Defence, HH Shaikh Muhammad bin Rashid al-Maktoum.

In Somalia, on Tuesday 20 January 1976, we had an official meeting with President Siad Barre in the presence of Emirati and Somali delegates.

HH Shaikh Zayed bin Sultan Al Nahyan had authorised me to offer aid to Somalia and support in establishing some vital projects as well as attempting to persuade Mr Barre away from Communism, an ideology which did not fit at all with the reality of the situation of our region.

During our visit, we saw different parts of Somalia during the day. In the evening, I had a number of meetings with Mr Barre and the translator was one of his ministers, Ahmed Hassan.

In one of those meetings, President Barre talked about Communism as a way of life. I objected, saying that 'An ignorant person is one who imports ideas from abroad, while it is a wise man who uses his own people's ideas and develops them.' When this was translated to him, he looked very angry and muttered some words in the Somali language which I did not understand.

At a later stage, when Ahmed Hassan fell out with Siad Barre, he visited me in Sharjah. I asked him about those words Siad Barre had said in our private meeting. 'Siad Barre was saying, "Cursed you are; cursed you are. You call me ignorant!"' Ahmed Hassan said.

On behalf of HH Shaikh Zayed bin Sultan Al Nahyan, I offered Somalia the following:

1. A $40,000,000 contribution from the State of the UAE to build a dam in Somalia;
2. Construction of a sugar factory;
3. Founding of three religious institutions to be run by the UAE Ministry of Education; and
4. Relief aid to those affected by the drought in Somalia.

A joint statement was prepared to this effect. However, when it was shown to President Barre he objected to the following passage in the document: 'The talks held confirmed the keenness of both countries to preserve the unity of the Islamic creed which brings the peoples of both countries together in accordance with the sublime principles of Islam. The talks also confirmed that both countries would work on strengthening those principles and fostering them by all possible means and in every way in order that the word of Allah might prevail.'

Since Mr Barre wanted this passage removed, I requested to meet him. I said, 'We, too, will have our own considerations regarding this statement.'

'Are you going to take back your offers of aid and the establishment of projects you made to Somalia?' he asked.

'This is not up to me. These are gifts from HH Shaikh Zayed bin Sultan Al Nahyan. When he authorised me to offer them, he did not place any conditions,' I replied.

'Fine. I approve the statement – as is – without any deletion,' he said.

Visit to Sudan

Following an earlier invitation by the Sudanese President Jaafar Nimeiry a visit was scheduled from 26 January until 30 January 1976. However, a day before we were to travel, Major Hassan Hussain Othman and twenty-two of his colleagues were executed for their part in the military coup of 5 September 1975 which involved 195 Sudanese Armed Forces personnel.

I returned to Sharjah from Somalia on 26 January 1976, and we said to the Sudanese here, 'You used to slaughter calves in honour of your guests. So, how is it that you are now slaughtering humans in honour of my arrival?'

Interviews with the Emirati and Kuwaiti press

I had a number of interviews with the press, the first of which was with both the Kuwaiti *al-Qabas* and the Emirati *al-Ittihād* newspapers at the same time. The interview appeared in the papers the next day, Saturday 6 March 1976:

Q: Your Highness, after this important stage in the history of the Emirates, what changes are there for the future of the country?

A: It is indeed a unique event in this region for seven Emirates to unite in one State after years of division and under-development. In only four years since our unification, we have managed to achieve so much. Even our concept of a Federation has gone through changes – to the extent that we are hearing calls for becoming all-in-one in a real and complete unity. This is due to the positive attitude and solidarity within all of us.

If we look at our provisional constitution, we can easily recognise the fact that the Federation began with an intent to bridge all viewpoints, to develop a well-informed strategy, and to create an entity that accommodates all the Emirates. If this experiment continues along the same lines that we have already undertaken, then the future holds great promise, not only for us, but also for the entire Gulf region and Arab nation.

Here in our country, we need to be more united than anywhere. Not all Arab countries have gone through a similar experience to ours. We hope that the unity we aspire to expands to include the entire Arab world from the Gulf to the Atlantic Ocean. Though it has only been four years, our advances exceed those of many other countries.

Prior to the establishment of our Federation, none of us had such responsibilities. Therefore, the experience has been both unique and new at the same time. The world is looking differently at us; our status in the international community has changed; we have established diplomatic relations with many countries, and joined many organisations and participated in many talks.

Previously, we were divided administratively – and every Emirate had its own local agencies, which were limited in scope of work and resources. If this were to have continued, this would have put an obstacle in the way of the progress of our Federation.

Experience showed that we had a severe shortage of professionals in various fields. In addition, the establishment of the laws and regulations for this State took a long time. However, at the present time, we pride ourselves on the fact that proper and solid grounds for progress in this country have been laid. Many great achievements have already been made, and we aspire to achieve much more.

Q: Your Highness, do you think there are internal disputes among the member Emirates in the Federation?

A: As I said earlier, our people were divided and are now united. Our country now has become one entity and has attained an elevated position. The people have high hopes as a result of this new-found unity and, as a result, we are not disposed to disputation. Our confederacy is different from any other; we are one people, made up of family members and relatives.

We took notice of the fact that citizens here demanded that no barriers of any kind should be placed in the way of their advancement, and we responded positively by promulgating the incorporation of all the local departments into Federal agencies, establishments and ministries. We have worked for – and in – the interests of the people and the region.

There are no disputes; though there are those who wish to stir up trouble. Still, my brothers, the Rulers are far-sighted and incorporation is indeed feasible. By the will of God, the people will soon witness the fruit of the efforts exerted for the benefit of this country.

Q: What about having one Federal army?

A: A military committee from Kuwait, Saudi Arabia and Jordan has already been formed to conduct a complete and comprehensive study regarding the military in the Emirates. It concluded its work last year and the findings were presented to the Supreme Council. Initial assent by their Highnesses, the Rulers, has also been given. A more thorough investigation is ongoing, and when the relevant committee reaches a final decision soon, it will be implemented. We shall all see that the benefits will affect the whole of the Emirates.

I had another interview with the Kuwaiti *Majalis* and the Emirati *al-Ittihād* newspapers. The interview was published in both papers on Friday 20 April 1976. In response to a question about progress towards Federation, I said:

The establishment of a Federation has been a new, as well as unique experience, as it took place in conditions that were not ideal owing to the artificial barriers that had been created by the colonialists as they withdrew, and by the divisions that surfaced at the time.

The Federation has already taken a great leap forward in terms of progress. However, there is a need for much greater experience in running the affairs of the Federation, internally and externally. We have had to face the fact that we did not have experience in running interior and foreign affairs at State level. Our previous experience was only at the level of the Emirate, while the foreign affairs and the like were run by the English. What has been achieved recently in this respect was in every way the direct result of having given the sons of this region – as well as its Rulers – the chance to gain the necessary experience.

In response to another question about how to overcome existing sensitive issues, I said: 'When State issues are evaluated, it is not unusual to have differing points of view. Agreements and disagreements are a must in order to reach what is of maximum benefit to the country. Also, any new experience cannot be expected to be free from negative aspects; the unity between Egypt and Syria was a clear example. It is, therefore, nothing unusual that differences should appear amongst people torn apart by colonialism.'

Asked to elaborate on this issue, I continued, saying: 'Just like a cyst can only be excised when it shows on the exterior of the skin, it is to our benefit to see the entire negativities surface. The experiences of European and other developed countries were free from similar negativities due to existing laws already in place over the years.'

Q: What about the provisional constitution?

A: The articles of the constitution were previously written corresponding to separate entities. The Ministry of Interior was more of a traffic department for highways. Today, the picture has changed, and the Ministry of Interior has started taking shape and is conducting its affairs as a true Ministry. Most Emirates have also already incorporated their security into that of the State – take for example al-Fujairah and 'Ajman.

On 16 April 1976, I announced in a meeting at another press conference:

Unity is our destiny and the true desire of the citizens of this region. The positions of some of the Emirates on certain issues in terms of the Federation indicate nothing other than their taking the time to reflect on the situation in order that our united march forward might be strong, and free from any negative approach. I should like to confirm that such positions are not obstacles or a kind of rejection to the idea of unity as some may wish to call it. Rather, there was a sincere desire from the members of the Supreme Council of the Federation – from the outset – that all steps taken should be appropriate, in order that the Federation might stand on firm ground.

I also said in an interview with the Chief Editor of the Kuwaiti *Sawt al-Khaleej* (Voice of the Gulf) that, 'The permanent constitution will contribute to strengthening the Federal foundations and will rid our country of the less positive aspects of the previous stage in a way that is in conformity with the aspirations of our people. There is no turning away from the unity of our people, especially considering that citizens have already been witnessing the benefits gained of late.'

Visit to Qatar

A scheduled short official visit to Qatar was arranged following an invitation by HH Shaikh Khalifah bin Hamad al-Thani, Emir of Qatar. Our journey started on 1 May 1976. The accompanying delegates were:

- HH Shaikh Abdullah bin Muhammad al-Qasimi, Head of the Emiri Diwan;
- His Excellency Shaikh Ahmad bin Sultan al-Qasimi, Minister of Justice;
- His Excellency Shaikh Saud bin Khalid al-Qasimi, Plenipotentiary at the Foreign Ministry;
- Shaikh Faisal bin Sultan al-Qasimi;
- Mr Taryam bin Imran bin Taryam, Ambassador of the UAE to Cairo;
- Mr Abdul-Rahman Bukhater, President of Sharjah National Bank; and
- Major Ali Fahd, Military Escort.

We arrived in Doha, Qatar, on the same day and were received by HH Shaikh Suhaim bin Hamad al-Thani, Foreign Minister of Qatar, and HH Shaikh Muhammad bin Jaber al-Thani, Minister of Municipal Affairs.

Immediately after our arrival in Doha, we had a meeting with HH Shaikh Khalifah bin Hamad al-Thani, Emir of Qatar. In the afternoon, we visited Qatar's National Museum and had a tour around Qatar afterwards. The following day, we left Doha for London on our way to the US.

Visit to America

The idea of my visit to the US came about after a conversation with Dr Ezzuddin Ibrahim, adviser to HH Shaikh Zayed bin Sultan Al Nahyan, President of the UAE. Dr Ibrahim told me that the Nation of Islam was an American organisation made up of people of African origin, and that they had converted to Islam under the direction of their leader, Elijah Muhammad.

Elijah is a word derived from the Arabic *Aali al-Jah* (of high status). It was given by Fard Muhammad, a Pakistani, as a title to 'Elijah Muhammad' when the latter became a Muslim. Three and half years later, Fard Muhammad disappeared. Elijah Muhammad then started making up his own rules and false stories about Islam. He even claimed to be a Messenger of God and that Fard Muhammad was indeed the Archangel Gabriel who had brought down the Qur'an to him. He also claimed that the white race was the Devil. After the death of Elijah Muhammad, his son, Warith-Uddin, took over and his understanding of Islam was much better than his father's had been. At the time under discussion, he desired to set the Islam of his organisation aright. But he was worried that some elements within the society were competing for the leadership of the organisation, among them Louis Farrakhan. 'So,' Dr Ezzuddin Ibrahim added, 'it is hoped that if you pay them a visit, this will enable Warith-Uddin to rectify the tenets of faith of the Nation of Islam and return them to the true and correct form of Islam.' I agreed to this mission and made the necessary arrangements for the visit, and Dr Ezzuddin would be meeting me there once the visit was under way.

On our way to the US, we spent one night in London, en route from Qatar, and then left for Chicago on 3 May 1976. That evening, at the airport in Chicago we were received by a huge crowd of 100,000 members of the Nation of Islam headed by Warith-Uddin, their leader. After we had shaken hands, garlands of flowers were placed around my neck as shouts of *Allahu Akbar* by the Muslims present filled the place.

At our reception, too, were Dr Ezzuddin Ibrahim, and Engineer Mostafa Mo'min, owner of Mo'min's office for Engineering Consultancy in Sharjah.

All the way from the airport to the hotel in which we were staying, the route was lined with crowds of Muslims running alongside the procession. The boxer Muhammad Ali (formerly Cassius Clay) was on the right side of my car, running with the crowds.

The roads became very busy thanks to all the people, the result of which was an hour-long traffic jam. The following day the press reported that there were many people who were not happy because of the traffic jam of the previous day.

The evening we arrived, arrangements were made to meet Warith-Uddin Muhammad in my hotel suite in the presence of Ezzuddin Ibrahim, who had arrived before me. When Warith-

Uddin came, Dr Ezzuddin Ibrahim said to him, 'I was just telling His Highness about the Nation of Islam.'

'My father,' Warith-Uddin said, 'learnt Islam from a layman, Fard Muhammad; and my father was the founder of this sect. I, however, noticed from a very early age that there were teachings that defied reason. And I do beg of you, Shaikh Sultan, to pave the way for me to announce the necessary changes.' I agreed, and we arranged to meet the next day.

On 4 May 1976, we visited the offices of the Nation of Islam to familiarise ourselves with the activities of the group. As we walked in the corridors between the offices, we were welcomed by all with the greeting of Islam, *Assalamu alaykum wa rahmatullahi wa barakatuh* (May the peace, mercy and blessings of Allah be with you).

In the afternoon, we met the group members in their mosque, which had formerly been a church that they had purchased and converted into a place of Islamic worship. It was in one of the most prominent streets in Chicago. It was a real surprise to us to find that their mosque was not a mosque at all in the traditional sense. Rather, it was laid out like the church it had once been, with lines of seats where the men and women of the Nation of Islam sat together. As for the podium, there were only rectangular seats on which we sat. Organised shouts of *Allahu Akbar* (God is Great) rang out.

The presenter, who was an Arab student from Sudan studying in Chicago, announced the beginning of the meeting, saying 'Holy Qur'an'. Then one of those present stepped forward and recited the first *Surah* of the Qur'an. When he reached the last word in the *Surah*, the entire hall echoed with 'Amen'.

Then the presenter introduced me to deliver the speech, the contents of which I had agreed with Warith-Uddin Muhammad the night before by way of helping him to introduce the required changes. I was to say that Elijah Muhammad was a Muslim Imam who had passed away before he could communicate the complete teachings of Islam, and that this task would be shouldered by his son and successor, Warith-Uddin Muhammad. I started by greeting them, and they all answered in one loud voice. I continued, 'Dear fellow Muslims, we are Muslims from the East. We have come here from over the seas, opening our arms to you in brotherhood. Your blood is as sacred and as inviolable as ours; so are your souls and honour. By Allah, whenever you call to us for help, you will find us at your side.'

At this, the entire hall burst into shouts of *Allahu Akbar*, and Warith-Uddin rushed to where I was sitting and tried to kiss my hand, but I pulled it away. He then threw himself on me and I had to hug him as he was sobbing and could be heard by all because the microphone was close to him. The congregation shouted repeatedly *Allahu Akbar*. I was jubilant, thinking they were cheering for me. However, I came to realise that that was not the case. The congregation was shouting because of something Elijah Muhammad had said previously – it seemed that what he had predicted had come true. My speech only made matters worse as Elijah Muhammad had told his followers that God was to send a messenger from the East to the Muslims in America. So, as I gave my speech, they assumed that I was the fulfilment of that prophecy!

Warith-Uddin then invited me to stand next to him as he addressed his group, saying, 'My fellow people, *our* Islam is not a complete Islam. The complete and true Islam is that of this

Shaikh.' He then raised my hand and continued, 'My father was not a messenger from God. He was no more than a Muslim Imam. As for Fard Muhammad, he was just a person from Pakistan that this Shaikh could have spoken to on the phone now, before you all.' I thought what he said was strange, as I had never known of this person.

Then Warith-Uddin added, 'My fellow people. Renew your Islam with me, and repeat: I bear witness that there is no god but Allah, and that Muhammad bin Abdullah bin Abdul-Muttalib, the Arab born in Arabia, is the Messenger of Allah,' and this they did. The meeting hall filled with shouts of *Allahu Akbar*, which only stopped after Warith-Uddin asked them to listen to the rest of his words.

'We will now go out to the court of the mosque to do the *Maghrib* prayer. So, let those who know how to perform *salah* join us; those who do not, you may do the same as we do, or watch us,' he said.

The direction of the *Qiblah* was determined, and the congregation stood in rows for the prayer. Dr Ezzuddin Ibrahim was urging me to lead the prayer and I was urging him to lead it himself. So, he said, 'I cannot do so. To them, I am the Devil because I am both white and blond!'

'This is a new day,' I said, 'and everything has changed.'

While praying with Dr Ezzuddin Ibrahim as our Imam, his loud recitation of the Qur'an thundered through the loudspeakers, and attracted multitudes of people from all the streets surrounding the mosque. They climbed over the walls of the mosque courtyard to watch the *salah* we performed that day in one of Chicago's major streets.

On 5 May 1976, the night before we left Chicago, I heard voices growing louder by the minute at the door of my suite in the hotel. I went over to find out what was happening. The tall young man at the door, Bilal Ajeeb, who was charged by the Nation of Islam to be my guard, informed me that the two men standing there wanted to see me, and that one of them was carrying a gun! I told him to let them in.

'We have been sent to you by Jim Jones, the founder and leader of the Peoples Temple,' one of them said. 'He is known for the building of Jonestown in 1974 to create a new socialist Eden on earth. He has avoided the media as they cause trouble. And he is saying that what he is doing might be a form of Islam. So, he is asking you to visit him and put him on the right track,' he added.

'I am the guest of Warith-Uddin Muhammad; so, if he approves your request, I will look into it,' I said.

Two years later, in November 1978, US Congressman Leo Ryan was leading a fact-finding mission to Jonestown in Guyana to investigate allegations of human rights abuses by Jones. He and some members of his entourage were assassinated by Jones's 'Red Brigade' at Georgetown airport. Immediately after this massacre, Jim Jones managed to convince more than nine hundred of his followers, including their children, to kill themselves using cyanide. This was the largest act of mass suicide in the history of the US. I wonder to this day if, had I visited that totally disturbed man, I could have done him some good.

A Muslim Brother!

On 6 May 1976 we set off from Chicago for San Francisco, where I had the honour of being presented with the keys to the city of San Francisco by its mayor. Afterwards, we visited California College, and spent one night there. The following day, we left San Francisco for Jacksonville.

On our way, at the invitation of the Governor of Tennessee, we stopped in Nashville and had lunch with the Governor in his house. As we sat at the table near which a girl was playing the harp, an African American man came from behind me to place a plate in front of me and whispered '*Assalamu alaykum wa rahmatullahi wa barakatuh*'.

I was intrigued by this man, so I watched him move around the room, in so doing not paying much attention to our host. Noticing this, he said, 'I can see you are intrigued by this employee. Is anything the matter?'

'No,' I replied.

'This employee is serving the last few days of a fifteen-year prison sentence following a murder in a bar. Some time ago, as is the custom in this state, I requested a houseman from the prison, and they told me he was a good-mannered person. He has been working here for the past six months. Prison transport brings him in the morning and collects him again in the evening. During his entire period here, he has never disobeyed an order, raised his voice, been caught snooping or touched money or a piece of jewellery. Do you know why? Because he is the leader of the Muslim prisoners!' the Governor said.

'As a Muslim he should be like this,' I replied.

At the threshold of the Governor's front door, the guests lined up to bid me farewell. That same employee rushed to open the car door for me. I held his arm and shook hands with him first, before doing so with the dignitaries. This seemed to annoy the Governor. As I sat next to him in the car on our way to the airport, he said disapprovingly, 'You turned away from the dignitaries and paid more attention to that worker!'

'He is my Muslim brother,' I said.

'You are a prince, and he is just a worker,' he said.

'Islam makes us equal,' I responded.

'Tell me about Islam,' he said.

'The best person to do so is that prisoner employee,' was my answer.

We went from Nashville to Jacksonville where we stayed at the house of my friend Mr Mason, the owner of numerous oil companies in America and abroad. He had sent his private aeroplane which had taken me and my accompanying delegates from Sharjah to Doha, then to London and the various US cities we travelled to, and then back to Sharjah. The house was beautiful and overlooked a wide river that flowed past the house.

On 8 May 1976 we headed for New York, and on the following day I visited David Rockefeller, who was running for the American presidency. On 10 May I met the UAE Ambassador to Washington, Mr Saeed Ghubash, together with some other Arab ambassadors. I also met Alfred Atherton, Assistant Secretary of State for Near Eastern and South Asian Affairs, and Senator James Abu Rizk, a man of Arab-Lebanese origin and a friend of mine. The next day, we left Washington for Belgium, where we stayed for one night before heading for Cairo on 12 May 1976.

Jawaher

On Friday 14 May 1976, I met my cousin's daughter, Jawaher bint Muhammad bin Sultan al-Qasimi in Cairo. She was a student in the Faculty of Arts at Cairo University. I proposed to her and she told me to speak to her father. So, on 16 May 1976, I left Cairo for Sharjah, and the following day spoke to Jawaher's father and asked him for his daughter's hand in marriage. He approved. On 22 July 1976, I married Jawaher bint Muhammad bin Sultan al-Qasimi in London. Together we have had three daughters, Budoor, Noor and Hoor and a son, Khalid. Jawaher has always been my helper, boon companion and supporter in times of hardship; and she remains so.

7

Zayed's Resignation

A S SOON AS I LANDED at Sharjah airport on 16 May 1976 on my return from Egypt, a huge crowd surrounded me to convey to me the good news of the unification of the various UAE Armed Forces, which was something I had called for previously. On Thursday 6 May 1976, while I was still in the USA, the Supreme Council for Defence announced the merger of all Armed Forces under one command and one flag.

That day, after the meeting chaired by HH Shaikh Zayed bin Sultan Al Nahyan, President of the UAE, the Council made a statement that the decision was taken as one of the steps to consolidate the Federal entity, and enhance its security and stability in order to be able to realise the hopes and aspirations of the people. By virtue of the decision of the Supreme Council for Defence,[14] all the land, sea and air forces of the UAE were to be put under one unified command called the Armed Forces General Command.

---

[14] Stipulated in Article 141 of the Constitution: 'A Supreme Council for Defence is to be established and headed by the president of the Federation'.

The statement made by the Council also defined the formation of the command of General Staff for a number of regions, namely the western military region, the central region, the northern region and the Yarmouk Brigade, which would incorporate all the Federal forces in Sharjah and Umm al-Quwain. Also named was the command for the air force, the navy and the main training institutes.

The leadership of the Armed Forces, and the responsibilities for these, were identified as follows: the President of the State was to be the Supreme Commander of the Armed Forces (air, land and navy). In his absence, the Vice-President would take command; and the Deputy Supreme Commander of the Armed Forces and Minister of Defence were to be jointly responsible directly to the President of the State in terms of running the military forces, its armaments and other material, leading all operations in defending the State and preserving the integrity of its land, air space and territorial waters against any external aggression, as well as maintaining the security, stability and unity of the State.

HH Shaikh Zayed bin Sultan Al Nahyan, President of the State and Chair of the Supreme Council of Defence, issued a decree regarding the powers of the General Chief-of-Staff. The decree designated the General Chief-of-Staff to be the adviser to HH, the President of the State, in military affairs.

By virtue of this decree, the General Chief-of-Staff was to implement the decisions of the Supreme Council for Defence, issue the commands and instructions thereof, devise the procedures for the procurement of armaments and equipment, provide for the development of the Armed Forces, propose necessary financial requirements in this regard and submit these to the

Minister of Defence for decision, take necessary measures for the organisation and training of the Armed Forces to ensure their capability to defend the State, ensure the readiness of the Armed Forces and raise their defensive capacity to the level of highest competence, prepare the cadres of officers and other ranks and files to take responsibility at all the various Armed Forces branches, and represent the State in all the conferences of the League of Arab States or any other external military meetings.

HH Shaikh Khalifah bin Zayed Al Nahyan was appointed Deputy Supreme Commander of the Armed Forces. Following a meeting with the Supreme Council for Defence, HH the President of the State issued a Federal decree to this effect. HH Shaikh Khalifah was entrusted with implementing the decisions of the Supreme Council of Defence in terms of organising, arming, preparing and equipping the Armed Forces.

HH Shaikh Zayed bin Sultan Al Nahyan, the President of the State, made a statement in which he talked about this historical step taken by the Supreme Council for Defence in unifying the Armed Forces of the UAE. Below, I quote substantial parts of HH's important speech on this historic event:

> With patience and perseverance, and with the help of the efforts of their Highnesses, the members of the Supreme Council of the Federation, we have managed on this historic occasion to achieve a dream that we have always had. We will not spare any effort in consolidating this Federal entity and enhancing its progress and stability. The hope we have always had was to establish a Federation that would bring us all together and strengthen our ties of blood and neighbourliness

in order to raise the standards of living for our people and real-ise all their aspirations. For the past five years, since the estab-lishment of the Federation, we have managed, with the help of God, to gain the requisite experience and to learn invaluable lessons that have enabled us to rectify the course of our march forward. The building of the Armed Forces in any country is a cherished and vital task for the people. That is why there has been a dire need to incorporate the various divisions of the Armed Forces of the UAE together.

Their Highnesses, the members of the Federal Supreme Council, have risen to the occasion and have proved their abili-ties in sharing the responsibility, in full understanding of the burden they are to shoulder. They have welcomed, with open arms, all the stages along the way to strengthening, advancing and supporting our Federal entity. This is a great achievement to add to our list of accomplishments and gains for us – and for all the people of this dear country of ours.

With hard work and perseverance, we will support all the efforts of the diverse departments of government involvement. This is, indeed, our duty and responsibility as leaders of the people. As we do so, we learn, at the same time, from the expe-rience and achievements of our brothers in both Arab and other friendly states. It is our duty not only to follow the exam-ple of our brothers, but also to avoid the mishaps and mistakes they have encountered. We need to take positive strides forward to achieve progress in all fields.

Referring to the incorporation of the police forces before, HH said:

His Highness Shaikh Sultan bin Muhammad al-Qasimi meets with Tunisian president Habib Bourguiba, March 1975.

His Highness Shaikh Sultan bin Muhammad al-Qasimi meets with the press following the announcement of historic decisions, November 1975.

Local masses that have supported the merger of the local councils into the Federal Ministries stand in front of the national assembly, November 1975.

A document from the British Library, no. 3725/12/LPS. *Left*, the al-Qawasim flag imposed on them by the British after defeat in 1820; *right*, the original al-Qawasim flag which the British lowered and replaced.

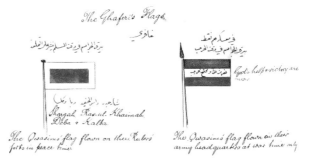

His Highness Sultan bin Muhammad al-Qasimi addresses the masses gathered in front of the national assembly to celebrate the merger of the local councils into the Federal Ministries, November 1975.

His Highness Shaikh
Sultan bin Muhammad
al-Qasimi raises the
Emirates' flag at the traffic
department building in
Sharjah, November 1975.

Raising of the Emirates'
national flag in front of
the national assembly in
Sharjah, November 1975.

His Highness Shaikh
Sultan bin Muhammad
al-Qasimi with the
President of Somalia,
Siad Barre, and Minister
Ahmed Hassan, January
1976.

His Highness
Shaikh Sultan
bin Muhammad
al-Qasimi with
His Excellency the
President of Sudan,
Jaafar Nimeiry,
January 1976.

His Highness Shaikh
Sultan bin Muhammad
al-Qasimi and the ruler
of Qatar, HH Shaikh
Khalifah bin Hamad al-
Thani, May 1976.

His Highness Shaikh Sultan bin Muhammad al-Qasimi during a visit to the offices of the Nation of Islam in Chicago, May 1976.

His Highness Shaikh Sultan bin Muhammad al-Qasimi delivers a speech before the Nation of Islam at their mosque in Chicago, a Sudanese interpreter by his side, May 1976.

Warith-Uddin Mohammed, leader of the Nation of Islam, delivers a speech at group's mosque in Chicago, May 1976.

His Highness Shaikh Sultan bin Muhammad al-Qasimi receives the key to the city of San Francisco from its mayor.

His Highness Shaikh Sultan bin Muhammad al-Qasimi on an exploratory visit to Khorfakan, 1976.

His Highness Shaikh Sultan bin Muhammad al-Qasimi celebrating the national day with His Highness Zayed bin Sultan Al Nahyan, 12 December 1976.

At Al Bahr Palace in Abu Dhabi with His Highness Shaikh Zayed bin Sultan Al Nahyan, 1976.

His Highness Shaikh Sultan bin Muhammad al-Qasimi receives Yemeni President Ibrahim al-Hamdi during his visit to the Sharjah Emirate, December 1976.

His Highness Shaikh Sultan bin Muhammad al-Qasimi meets with President Hafez Al Assad, March 1977.

His Highness Shaikh Sultan bin Muhammad al-Qasimi and His Highness Zayed bin Sultan Al Nahyan after the approval of the Emirates budget, June 1977.

The police force is one of the cornerstones for the stability and security of this land. We have already managed to unify our police forces. And today, we add another achievement for the protection of our nation and the consolidation of its security; that is, the Armed Forces. Both the police and the army represent the two arms of our nation; in the absence of one, the other is weak. And when both are there, strong and united, the people will feel that their lives, honour and wealth are properly protected.

Previously, we depended on the experience of many in a variety of different fields; but we understand the necessity of education for our own children since we desperately need them. In spite of the short period of time since the establishment of the Federation, we have managed to deploy our human resources in the best possible way in many of the State's organisations. The dedication and loyalty of our children in performing their national duties is nothing but exemplary.

HH concluded by saying that, 'Their Highnesses, the members of the Supreme Council of the Federation, have already overcome many difficulties and have shouldered their responsibilities admirably with all sincerity of purpose and intention. They are all determined to continue working towards realising the hopes and dreams of the people in all fields.'

The reactions to this historical decision of incorporating the Armed Forces were exceptionally positive – with all the official bodies, as well as the general public, rejoicing in the decision, and describing it as a pioneering step forward in support of Federal unity.

Unity is a National Request

Commenting on these dramatic developments, and in an interview published in the *Manar al-Islam* magazine on 27 May 1976, I said the following:

> Unity is the goal of everyone. Small entities have no place among nations. We are working towards strengthening our Federation through the propagation of the value of unity, and encouraging all to reject differences and disunity. All the existing entities need to merge into one nation so that we can all work in the interests of the general public, and not merely for the benefit of specific individuals.
>
> Sharjah, for example, being part of the UAE, interacts with the Federation and plays an important role that is apparent to all. We have been the active part of the Federation at both the institutional and public levels. Most of our local departments have already been integrated within Federal institutions, and this is only one part of Sharjah's contribution to the Federation.

In response to a question about how to strike a balance between the revenues generated from oil production and the preservation of our Islamic heritage and ethics, I stated that, 'If oil wealth is used well, it will be the means to raise the standard of living of the people. As for our Islamic ethics and morals, these are not things that dissipate or go away, especially if we have our children growing up with our heritage and have always taken steps to preserve it. So, oil could be utilised in the service of our heritage and help us to achieve wonderful results in this regard.'

Dealing with the issue of the growing relations between the UAE and foreign countries, I commented: 'The UAE is a country loyal and giving with friends and is likewise with all other countries, too. We have reached a level of international relations that is praiseworthy.'

As for protecting our youth against atheistic currents, I said, 'If their minds are informed and not idle, then there is no distorted thought that could overcome the minds of our youth. Here in the Arab and Islamic world, we are principled people of strong faith and belief, based on divine revelations, before which all man-made dogmas are powerless.'

I also commented on the importance of giving required attention to Islamic *Da'wa* (preaching) saying, 'Three elements need be available to realise required goals in this regard: competent men with relevant experience who are sincere in their efforts for the sake of Islamic *Da'wa*; proper use of the mass media in the service of *Da'wa*; and working towards infusing the spirit of collective and committed effort for the sake of Islamic *Da'wa* in our children in the schools and kindergartens.'

Constitution of the United Arab Emirates

The provisional constitution had been signed on 18 July 1971, by all the Rulers of the Emirates except for Ras al-Khaimah, whose Ruler, Shaikh Saqr bin Muhammad al-Qasimi, abstained, believing his country could develop better terms under which it would join. That was the reason Article 152 was added, stating: 'This Constitution shall take effect from the date to be fixed in a declaration to be issued by the Rulers who are signatories to this

Constitution.' The aforementioned declaration was proclaimed in Dubai on 2 December 1971. Ras al-Khaimah eventually joined the Federation on 10 February 1972 and its admission to the State of the UAE meant its implicit acceptance of the provisional constitution.

On 21 February 1976, the Supreme Council met and reviewed the report of the founding committee charged with preparing the draft of the permanent constitution. The Council commissioned the committee to work on the final phrasing of the constitution and to submit it by 9 March 1976. The Council also instructed the National Federal Council to convene a special session for the discussion of the permanent constitution.

In the March 1976 meeting of the Supreme Council, the amendments made by the founding committee were approved, and, as a result, the permanent constitution was ready to be discussed by the National Federal Council. In the special session held to discuss the permanent constitution, some members added a number of articles to it. Prominent among them were an article that would have given legislative powers to the National Federal Council, and another that would have given the Federal government the authority over all local matters in all the Emirates. Some members started misinforming the general public, saying that certain Rulers were placing obstacles in the path of the new draft, and were dismissive of the amendments.

In view of this situation, I was obliged to respond to such rumours. So, on 16 April 1976, I spoke to the press. 'Unity is our destiny and sincere hope,' I said.

No one is against the incorporation and consolidation of the Federal institutions. The stand taken by some Emirates regarding some of the Federal issues is merely conjectural. Their objective is that our way forward be forthright, clear and free from all negativities. As such, they are not obstacles or a kind of rejection as some would like to call them. Rather, they are manifestations of a sincere desire on the part of the members of the Supreme Council that the steps taken should be appropriate and well thought through. The newly drafted permanent constitution will contribute to strengthening the foundations of the Federation and will put an end to any negative aspects of the past stage.

On Monday 12 July 1976, the Supreme Council of the Federation met to discuss the draft of the permanent constitution. There were three main options to discuss: first, to approve the draft of the permanent constitution as submitted by the founding committee and to reject the amendments of the National Federal Council. This, however, would result in a bad reaction on the part of citizens vis-à-vis the Rulers; second, to approve the draft of the permanent constitution with the inclusion of the amendments suggested by the National Federal Council. This, however, would hinder, if not stop altogether, operations nationwide, especially considering that some of the existing institutions and departments were local, while others were national, and considering that the Federal State agencies were not yet competent enough to run them efficiently; or, third, to extend the transitional term of the UAE provisional constitution.

The Supreme Council of the Federation unanimously agreed to the third option, and issued a decree stating: 'On this day, Monday 12 July 1976, the Supreme Council of the Federation has decided to extend the transitional term of the UAE provisional constitution for another five calendar years commencing the second day of December 1976.'

Shaikh Zayed Resigns

In early August 1976, news spread among the people that HH Shaikh Zayed was to step down as President of the Federation. This piece of news was published in the Bahraini *Akhbar al-Khaleej* (Gulf News) after its Editor-in-Chief met HH Shaikh Zayed on Saturday 31 July 1976. Shaikh Zayed had made a statement that included his refusal to renew his Presidency of the Federation of the Emirates for another five years starting December 1976. The newspaper stated that this was in accordance with a decision made by the Supreme Council of the Federation in its last session on Monday 12 July, where it was also decided that the status of the provisional constitution should be extended for a similar period. Shaikh Zayed's decision came as a surprise to everyone, including the senior officials of the State as well as to us, the members of the Supreme Council.

It was obviously untrue that Shaikh Zayed's decision not to renew his Presidency for another five years had been taken by the Supreme Council of the Federation in its latest session of 2 July 1976. Nothing regarding HH stepping down had been discussed during the session. *Akhbar al-Khaleej* should have said that Shaikh Zayed had made his own decision in the Supreme Council of the

Federation, linking his decision to step down with the decision to extend the term of the provisional constitution.

Such a statement would have shown that Shaikh Zayed's decision was based primarily on various members' rejection of the permanent constitution draft – to which Shaikh Zayed himself had devoted significant effort – a draft which would have allowed Shaikh Zayed to be fully empowered to shoulder the broad responsibilities of the Presidency.

During that period, the members of the Supreme Council were in constant contact with one another in an attempt to contain this political crisis. On Wednesday 4 August 1976, however, the *al-Ittihād* newspaper had on its front page: 'Zayed insists on stepping down. Sources confirm that the President of the State will not accept the extension of his Presidency under the current circumstances.'

The next day, Thursday 5 August 1976, HH Shaikh Zayed, President of the State, was at Abu Dhabi airport, heading for Somalia on a special visit for a week. From there, he was to head to Sri Lanka to attend the Non-Aligned States Conference starting on 16 August 1976. Shaikh Zayed's visit to Somalia had not been planned. He had made the decision to visit Somalia at that particular time so we did not have the chance to meet with him to dissuade him from his decision to step down and so that we, the Supreme Council, might realise that we had made a mistake by making a hasty decision to extend the transitional term of the provisional constitution, even though it still had four months to run.

Shaikh Zayed was away for thirty-four days, which, for me, felt like an age. The whole of the UAE felt like a desolate place, and the public was waiting for his return in desperate anticipation.

On Thursday 9 September 1976, thousands of people from all over the country gathered in a public demonstration in Abu Dhabi airport to receive Shaikh Zayed as he returned. They were holding signs bearing slogans that read:

— *Welcome back, Zayed.*
— *We are all with you.*
— *We won't give up the leader of our march forward.*
— *Your Presidency of the Federation is a source of strength to us and all Arabs.*
— *We want no one else but Zayed.*
— *We are for you, Zayed, herald of welfare.*
— *No! No! No stepping down!*
— *Rulers! Strength is in Unity.*
— *We will defend you with our lives.*

In the midst of all this, a reporter from *al-Ittihād* came to ask me how I felt about this, and so I said:

The people of the UAE are all in agreement that Zayed should stay as leader of our march towards Federation now and in the future. My sincere hope is that the President of the State will change his mind regarding his decision to step down. We do not want anyone else, and want him not to leave us at the critical period we are currently experiencing. All the people in the UAE have the hope that Zayed will continue to lead the way forward for the next term, and for many terms to come, *inshallah*. We are all behind him with our support, and we pray that Allah might grant him success in all his efforts towards unifying this nation and achieving all that pertains to the welfare of the people and of the country as a whole.

No sooner had HH Shaikh Zayed stepped out of his plane than the voices coming from all directions inside and outside the airport spontaneously echoed in unison and harmony: 'Zayed, Zayed, Zayed'. Shaikh Zayed got into his car and passed through the enveloping crowds and he headed for the al-Butain Palace followed by a train of cars. When we went into the palace, the crowds had already gathered round it and we could hear the voices coming at us from all directions. At this moment, Shaikh Zayed ordered that the doors of the palace be opened to let the crowds in. Everyone came rushing in wanting to embrace him.

On the evening of the next day, 10 September 1976, a statement from the *Diwan* of HH, President of the State, was issued expressing the appreciation of the President to the people and thanking them for their expressions of love and loyalty. The statement read:

> We are honoured to convey to our people the most sincere thanks and feelings of appreciation for their expression of loyalty they conveyed to HH, the President of the State, upon his return home the day before yesterday. HH, the President of the State, has viewed the letters and telegrams sent him by our citizens and has followed what has been published in the local and Arab newspapers as regards the concerns and aspirations of this nation.
>
> Our people have proven, in the light of current events, that they are positive in their outlook, have a high sense of

awareness, and are keen for the State to maintain its unity and the unity of its citizens.

HH, the President of the State, is very pleased to express his loyalty to the people who showered him with their love, provided him with their support, backed him up with their trust in appreciation of his sacrifices and his efforts towards the creation of our young State, the consolidation of its status and the confirmation of its national identity. This great people has shown a real desire to maintain the unity and cohesion of the State, and a relentless determination to remove all obstacles from its way forward.

HH, the President of the State, wishes to thank the people most sincerely for their warm expression of feelings, for their show of solidarity and for their insistence that we move forward in our endeavours to achieve distinction and welfare for all.

In this blessed month, we pray to Allah, the Almighty, to guide us all towards what is right and pray that His Highness's desires and wishes for his people to advance and prosper be granted.

And say, 'Do [as you will], for Allah will see your deeds, and [so, will] His Messenger and the believers.' [Qur'an]

On the morning of Saturday 18 September 1976, I visited HH Shaikh Zayed in Abu Dhabi. The meeting was to convince him to change his mind about stepping down as President. Present at the meeting was His Excellency, Foreign Minister, Ahmed bin Khalifah al-Suwaidi.

The next day I also visited HH Vice-President Shaikh Rashid bin Sa'id al-Maktoum, in Dubai, and talked to him about persuading HH Shaikh Zayed not to step down.

On Monday 20 September 1976, HH Shaikh Rashid bin Sa'id al-Maktoum visited me in Sharjah and informed me that he was going to visit HH Shaikh Zayed in Abu Dhabi to convey to him the insistence and consensus of the Rulers that he continue to be the leader and remain as President of the Federation. HH Shaikh Rashid bin Sa'id al-Maktoum visited him two days later. It was agreed during their meeting that this issue be left to the discussions of the Supreme Council of the Federation.

Spirit of Responsibility and Understanding

The meeting of the Supreme Council on Saturday 6 November 1976 was dominated by a spirit of responsibility and understanding, with a number of preliminary and pilot meetings preceding it. The overarching aim would be the preservation of the confederation, the conceptualisation of the next important stage and working towards achieving the security and stability of the country and welfare of our people.

The Council examined the report of HH, the President of the State, regarding the requirements of the next stage, and the following decisions were approved:

First, issuance of a constitutional amendment to the effect that the provision of Article 142 of the UAE provisional constitution would be revoked in order that only the State itself shall have the right to establish land, sea and air armed forces.

Second, issuance of a decision granting the President the right to overall supervision, through Federal agencies, of all matters relating to immigration, residency, maintenance of State-wide law and order, and monitoring the nation's shores, border posts, ports and airports in order to prevent illegal entry into the country, and to secure the country's national integrity.

Third, issuance of a Federal law to set up the Department of State Security under the direct headship of the President of the State, so that the intelligence sections and all other local agencies operating in member Emirates and conducting intelligence work would be incorporated into the aforementioned State Security Department.

Fourth, dealing with the administration of the Ministry of Information and Culture, the information stated that the Minister of Information and Culture would retain full authority to supervise and politically direct the work of radio and TV in the UAE. The Ministry would be responsible for the accreditation of political and news materials, and for reviewing all news bulletins, political programmes and comments, talks and news relating to the policies of the State internally and externally, prior to their broadcast. The Ministry of Information and Culture would retain the right to unify the broadcast of the news bulletins from the various radio channels of the State on the same frequency. The decision also stipulated that all broadcasts from the State's radio and TV channels emphasise the unity of the State by mentioning, in each instance, the name of the State before that of individual Emirates and in accordance with the instructions of the Minister of Information and Culture.

Fifth, all Emirates were to contribute to the annual budget of the Federation in light of the estimates of the Federal budget proposal of 1977 which would be submitted to the Supreme Council. A committee was to be formed to discuss and determine the general framework of the State's general budget for the year 1977 in light of the needs submitted by the Federal ministries and departments. The aforementioned committee would submit its findings to the Supreme Council of the Federation. This committee had HH Shaikh Sultan bin Muhammad al-Qasimi, Member of the Supreme Council and Ruler of Sharjah, as its head. The members of the committee were HH Shaikh Hamad bin Muhammad al-Sharqi, Member of the Supreme Council and Ruler of al-Fujairah, HH Shaikh Hameed bin Rashid al-Nu'aimi, Crown Prince of 'Ajman, and the members of the Ministerial Committee for Financial Affairs.

Sixth, postponement of the discussion of the issue of unresolved internal borders between the different Emirates in order to complete current negotiations, and following up the results of efforts to reach a final settlement on this issue.

The Supreme Council also approved the recommendations of the Saudi Security Mission to set up a General Directorate for Civil Defence tasked with protecting the people and public and private properties, aiding the victims of natural disasters, securing the means of transportation, ensuring the smooth operation of public utilities and guarding national assets during times of war, emergency and general disasters. The General Directorate for Civil Defence, incorporating at the same time the various fire brigades in member Emirates of the Federation, was to become one of the main departments of the Ministry of Interior, and was required to conduct its tasks and duties nationwide. The decision also stated that a training institute for civil defence purposes would be established and be provided with the required human, physical and technical resources necessary to enable the General

Directorate for Civil Defence and its branches to conduct their work with efficiency and effectiveness.

The following Federal bills and decrees were also approved: setting up a *Diwan* for State Auditing; setting up a system for pensions and military retirement awards; promulgating a corpus of Juvenile Law; approving an agreement to set up the Arab Satellite Communications Organisation; and approving technical cooperation for industrial development in the UAE.

The final important decision that was taken during the Supreme Council meeting was to hold the election of the President of the State and his Vice-President, for the next term commencing 2 December 1976, at the next session of the Supreme Council on Saturday 27 November of the same year. The Supreme Council also stated that it hoped for a prosperous future during which the Federation and its citizens might achieve their aspirations for unity, progress and self-respect in the ensuing stages and that Allah might guide all to achieving the best for the nation.

In accordance with the above, on Saturday 27 November 1976, the Supreme Council of the Federation met. HH Shaikh Zayed bin Sultan Al Nahyan was elected President of the UAE, and HH Shaikh Rashid bin Sa'id Al-Maktoum was elected Vice-President of the State.

8

Early Days as Ruler of Sharjah

My DAILY AND WEEKLY SCHEDULE has always been, especially since the early days of ruling Sharjah, very busy. In those early days, Saturdays used to be particularly consuming. Every Saturday morning, there was a general *majlis* in the headquarters of the Sharjah government to meet the locals who, be they nationals or otherwise, came from all over Sharjah. I would be there listening to their problems and trying to solve them. Although such meetings were very tiring for me personally and for the employees and security guards alike, I enjoyed them very much because they kept me close to my people. Other consuming and frequent activities included inspection rounds in the eastern region, namely Daba, Khor Fakkan Kalbaa, Dhaid, Maliha, Mudam and Hamriyya; inspection rounds to governmental institutions and departments to ensure work was being conducted satisfactorily; and visits to work sites of the projects undertaken by the Government of Sharjah.

I carried out a number of broader political, cultural and social activities in those days and I will elaborate on a few of them below.

Symposium on Arab-African Relations

On Tuesday 14 December 1976, I inaugurated the Arab-African Symposium held in the Africa Hall in Sharjah in which forty-five Arab and African intellectuals participated. The discussions revolved round Arab-African relations and the best means to effect cooperation between the respective countries. The symposium concluded its work on Saturday 18 December 1976 by adopting a resolution that set up the Documentation and Data Collection Centre for Arab-African Relations. The headquarters of the Centre was to be in Sharjah.

The symposium chose me as Honorary President of the Centre. This was the first recommendation of the symposium as it concluded its sessions. The symposium also recommended that a meeting be held annually in December to continue investigating, researching and studying Arab-African relations.

The symposium also called upon all African and Arab countries to develop a new strategy to deal with the issues of economic cooperation between them, that permanent joint cooperation institutions be established, and that the Charters, rules and regulations of the League of Arab States and Organisation of African Unity be reviewed to enable both bodies to interact effectively with new realities and events.

The symposium also recommended increased support for academic and specialised establishments, institutes and universities as well as increased encouragement of studies and exchange of students and cultural exchange.

It also called for setting up a joint African Arab Fund to support and assist national liberation movements in Africa and the Arab world. In addition, it stressed its conviction that progress and development required intensive effort to enhance the awareness of human rights and to promote equality.

The Sharjah declaration included a number of important principles, mainly that the Arab and African peoples share a deeply rooted historical and cultural heritage, and have a shared struggle against oppressive powers. Therefore, it was clear that the future of the peoples of Africa and the Arab world would be strongly connected in tangible ways.

For my part, I sent these recommendations to Arab Kings and Presidents who, around that time, were going to attend the Arab summit at the League of Arab States.

The Fifth UAE National Day

On Sunday 12 December 1976, a national celebration was held in Abu Dhabi for the fifth National Day, which included a military parade and a huge cultural festival. Attending were the President of the State and the members of the Supreme Council of the Federation.

That day, the President addressed the nation saying that, 'The burden of the trust I am shouldering is indeed heavy. We all need to be together in perfect unity to be able to build the future of our country, to achieve a high standing for our nation, and to realise our dreams.'

Addressing the members of the Supreme Council after thanking them for his re-election as President, HH Shaikh Zayed said, 'I consider this trust a huge responsibility as well as an honour. However, I can only undertake it with the help of

Allah, and the support of my brothers (the Rulers) and the people as a whole.'

Visit of the Yemeni President, Ibrahim al-Hamdi

On the morning of Sunday 19 December 1976, President Ibrahim al-Hamdi, President of the Command Council of the Arab Republic of Yemen, arrived in Sharjah on a one-day visit, after which he was to travel to Beijing at dawn on Monday 20 December 1976.

We met and held talks and had a lunchtime banquet in his honour with Sharjah dignitaries attending. The Yemeni President also met with the Yemeni community at Government House and he talked to them about the efforts the Yemeni government had made with regard to the advancement and development of Yemen.

The Opening of the Sharjah Da'wa Centre

The Sharjah Da'wa Centre was inaugurated on Tuesday 21 December 1976, in the presence of Mr Warith-Uddin Muhammad, the leader of the Nation of Islam group in the US, and whom I had met the year before in Chicago.[15] That day, a decision was made to produce a translation of the Qur'an in English, and to get it recorded on tape so that English speakers in the States and other English-speaking countries might have access to the Qur'an and its correct interpretation. Consequently,

---

[15] See Chapter 6.

I formed a committee chaired by Dr Ezzuddin Ibrahim with the membership of the Sharjah Radio Station Director, Saeed Imara, the Sharjah Radio presenters Saad Ghazal and Mahmoud al-Shareef, in addition to Dr Muhammad Mostafa al-A'zami from Syria. Then we chose the English translation entitled 'The Meaning of the Glorious Qur'an' by Mohammad Marmaduke Pickthall as the one to be used for the purposes of the project. Dr Muhammad Mostafa al-A'zami made many corrections to Pickthall's translation, then the Arabic audio recording of the Qur'an was made in Greece, while the English audio recording was carried out in London. The task of putting the two together was done in Sharjah. We were all so pleased when the distribution of the audio tapes began in early September 1977.

Visits to Sharjah Schools

I have always believed that education should be given top priority; this is a belief that I have striven to translate into reality from schools to universities. In those early days I kept a close eye on our schools in Sharjah, and as part of that remit I visited them now and then. In 1976 I decided to arrange a tour around many of those schools, starting on Saturday 25 December 1976. The first day, I went to al-Uruba Secondary School for Boys, and Fatima al-Zahraa' Secondary School for Girls. The next day, I visited intermediate schools, among which was the Ali bin Abi Talib School. On my visits, I was accompanied by His Excellency, the Minister of Education, Abdullah bin Imram bin Taryam.

During my meetings with the students, I spoke openly and frankly, answered their questions and discussed the issues they presented to me. Those meetings revealed how eager the students were to find out the truth about critical and crucial issues the UAE had to encounter.

The topics tackled varied. I spoke, for example, about the Federation, saying that,

> undoubtedly our Federal march forward has encountered many challenges as a result of old practices that were contrary to the new reality. As a result, the first two years were particularly difficult. Each Emirate had continued to follow old practices, something which needed getting rid of. However, the State managed to undertake its natural role. As time went by, conflicting rules and regulations surfaced and caused our way forward to stall to some extent. Yet, one must admit that forming a Federation is a positive act that allows us to overcome obstacles and push ahead with vigour.
>
> We learned that the appearance of problems and conflicts at a very early stage should not be something to fear since this makes them easy to deal with and find adequate solutions before it is too late. To cite an example, it is much better to treat a superficial skin problem quickly and effectively before it gets worse and requires limb amputation. Early treatment of problems accumulated since the times of colonialism and occupation makes our progress easily achievable.

On the role of the youth, I said, 'You are required to help propagate the concept of unity everywhere. We do not believe, however, that establishing a Federation is the ultimate goal for the youth. In fact, it is the starting point towards a comprehensive unity. As youth, you need to understand fully the concept of a unity which is built on rock-solid foundations and then to acknowledge the reason why this is important.'

I also addressed the issues relating to the status of women and their representation in the National Council. 'Women in our country are undervalued, but are demanding equality, which we have no objection to,' I said.

On the contrary, we encourage such calls and support them. When a woman has founded her Arab and Muslim character on firm foundations, she is worthy of her rights. Nations all over the world have got used to the fact that freedoms and rights are taken, not given.

As for representation of women [in the National Council], it is an undeniable fact that there are deeply-rooted customs and traditions in our society that we have to be careful about. In Europe itself, representation of women is still very limited and women representatives can be counted on two hands. So, we are not the exception. There are, however, many other ways for women to achieve their desired goals. When the obstacles to the present stage are overcome, women will be able to move to the next. Our religion strongly supports women realising all their legitimate rights.

I also expressed my optimism about the new Cabinet, saying, 'Our way forward will gain momentum in the coming years when old obstacles are overcome. We will also hold ourselves accountable at the end of the coming stage and examine what we have achieved for our country. We are not blaming everything that is wrong on the previous Cabinet, since present shortcomings could also be the result of the conflicts between the reality on the ground and the newly introduced Federal legislations.'

On public awareness, I said, 'I wish for the new generations to be better equipped in knowledge, faith and love for their country. We are seeking to produce young people of the kind who can shoulder the responsibility of leading the Federation and facilitating its progress to a higher stage of evolution and development. To get there, the youth, in their learning and knowledge, need to achieve ever higher levels to accommodate to the realities of our modern age.'

On university study, I said, 'It is very pleasing to see our young daughters raising the banner of learning and joining universities to seek higher education. As for the young men who are pursuing their studies in various universities abroad, they are required to represent their country in the best possible manner, develop their characters and act as true men of this land.'

I also responded to questions about the budget submitted to the Supreme Committee and how prepared the Emirates were to contribute, saying:

The Financial Committee is continuing its efforts to develop solutions for existing problems so that we can move forward.

Although the general budget is huge, reaching 14.5 billion dirhams, levels of expenditures are still very high. The Committee will try to control these levels in ways that serve public interest the most. Part of the budget will be allocated for external aid and another for internal projects.

The fact is that only 40–60 per cent of previously planned

projects have been completed. As a result, the development of the State agencies has not been in tune with the requirements of the new stage of expansion. This means that the most important task for the new Cabinet is to execute all previously agreed projects.

I also added, 'At present, the State has twenty-one thousand employees, and is in need of another ten thousand more for the next year. Yet, recruiting will not be conducted following the methods of the past. It is going to be different so that it guarantees gaining the most benefit from employees' efforts and productivity.'

As for the contributions of the various Emirates to the coming general budget, I stated that 'All the Emirates were to contribute to it following the example of Abu Dhabi, which took a pioneering step in this regard and has shouldered alone the burden of the budget during the past five years. Abu Dhabi has already committed itself to contribute 50 per cent of its revenues to the upcoming budget. In addition to this, the President of the State, HH Shaikh Zayed bin Sultan Al Nahyan, had contributed more than this.'

I also commented on the continuing discussions on constitutional affairs, stating that they should not block the aspirations of the people to realise more Federal gains since there was a strong public desire to achieve unity. 'When efforts to develop a permanent constitution were unsuccessful, we extended the transitional term of the provisional constitution to give ourselves time to resolve the outstanding issues,' I added. 'If we look closely, however, we can easily see that many of the articles in the constitution have already been amended. Ardent, dedicated young people should not consider extending the transitional term of the UAE provisional constitution to be a discouraging step. The younger generation needs to develop the insight to see that their interests will be better served when comprehensive unity is achieved.'

As regards the unsettled border problems, I explained that 'there should not be any fear when little problems emerge at this stage. It is better that we deal with such issues very early before they get worse and become irreparable.' I also stated that, 'the brothers [Rulers] are capable of solving such issues among themselves. This is emphasised by the fact that the borders in question are no more than a few kilometres inland. The need to reach a solution is ineluctable, and yielding to logic is inescapable.'

I went on explaining to the students that 'the current disputes are remnants of what colonial powers had left us with. The aim was to lumber us with problems after their departure so that they could achieve the objectives of their own hidden agendas.' I added, 'The colonial powers were deeply aware of how strategically important this region is in terms of its wealth. Therefore, they have been deliberately driving wedges between the brothers at State level and in the Arab world as a whole. By contrast, we see that the colonialists did not impose the imperative for division on India, for example, as they realised that India was not as "giving" as the Arab countries would be.'

In addition, I also spoke about the new Cabinet stating that 'the Prime Minister has the right to form his new Cabinet the way he sees fit and in accordance with members' competence and not be restricted by previously held ministerial posts. Hence, my great hope is that the new Cabinet will be able to move forward much more easily and infuse our efforts with a sense of positive endeavour.'

Responding to a question about the increase in the numbers of expatriates, I said:

> True, the numbers of expatriates have recently gone up. However, no matter how many more are required, this should not pose a threat to the State, especially since using expatriates is only a transitional solution until major projects have been executed. At that point, those expatriates who are not required will leave. The Ministry of Labour has recently attempted to recruit a cadre of Arab workers and experts. But, the problem has been that securing Arab manpower has been more difficult than before owing to competition emanating from neighbouring countries.

On the issue of the wastage of State funds and profiteering by some senior officials, I stated, 'The coming period will witness a radical change in regard to such issues. A new evaluation system will be in place in every ministry so that all State employees will be held accountable for their actions in order that all acts of foul play might be exposed.' I also added, 'We are aware of the illicit gains that some have made from State funds. However, the upcoming phase will leave no room for this small handful of offenders to continue as before.'

A question was posed regarding the negative attitude of some groups towards the Palestinian cause. By way of response, I said,

The Palestinian cause is a focal point in our struggle. Had it not been there, we would not have endeavoured to unite and band together to fight colonialism. The Palestinian cause may be considered a rallying point for us all. It does not only concern the Palestinians alone; rather, it is the cause of the entire Arab nation. We have to make it known that we are willing to sacrifice our lives for this cause and this is our stated position. The ambitions of Israel go beyond the borders of Palestine and may expand forward to encompass a far greater area, and because of this we keep thinking of Arab unity in the fight against colonialism.

In response to another student's question whether it was necessary to build many airports, harbours and the like in the various parts of the country, I said,

The region has been witnessing rapid developments coupled with an increase in population and the emergence of large, dynamic, commercial and industrial enterprises. These have necessitated that we expand in all areas, including the construction of airports and ports. We fully realise that such facilities represent a key feature in the development of the country – something which we have definitely accomplished to date. Added to this is the fact that the increased desire to travel to and within this region is bound to bring us closer together in the sense that Abu Dhabi, Dubai and Sharjah will become more intimately connected. This will necessarily entail coordinating the efforts of the Emirates within the State.

A student from al-Zahraa' Secondary School for Girls asked about the possibilities of establishing a comprehensive Arab unity and what the requirements would be to achieve this end. I answered, saying that, 'As far as the Arab world is concerned, the colonial powers endeavoured to divide it and dismember it into disputing fragments in spite of the fact that they did not do this elsewhere. The reason was their realisation that our lands are rich, incorporate four important straits and comprise all the necessary elements for successful economic integration.' I then went on to say,

These elements may be added to the presence of further grounds for unity manifest in the fact that we share one history, one language and one deeply rooted religion. Are these in themselves not sufficient basis for establishing a comprehensive unity?

If we look at the European countries, we will see that they started to work collectively as a bloc. They have succeeded in becoming a united power and active force in world affairs despite the fact that they lack what is available to us in the Arab world in terms of unifying factors and shared religion, language and history.

As for when and how Arab unity may be achieved, we are at a stage in Arab history that is characterised by stagnation. Perhaps, this is the calm that comes before the storm. Our hope is that more concerted and active effort will be made for us, as a family, to work together.

I then addressed the notion of how Arab unity could be realised, saying,

> Previously, the thinking was that such a unity could become a reality by force or by means of occupation or bilateral relations. However, it seems to me that the best way to realise the aspirations of the Arab masses is to change the Charter of the League of Arab States so that, from this moment on, this organisation might work towards facilitating economic and industrial integration, the unification of education systems, as well as the unification of all Arab armies.

I continued to the effect that, 'In spite of the fact that colonial powers seemed to have shaped all Arab countries in different and disharmonious ways – especially when we look at the influence of the French and English languages – this problem may be easily overcome by giving every Arab state a kind of autonomy or self-rule as in the case of the United States of America.' I concluded by expressing my optimism that 'such unity will soon become a reality at the hands of our youth, especially when our young people are able to foster, in themselves and in others, the concept of unity'.

The Death of Shaikh Muhammad bin Sultan al-Qasimi

The year 1977 did bring with it some sad events as well. On Saturday 5 February, Shaikh Muhammad bin Sultan al-Qasimi, the former Minister of Labour, passed away. On Monday 7 February, I headed the funeral procession together with the Ruler of Ras al-Khaimah, Shaikh Saqr bin Muhammad al-Qasimi; the Crown Prince of 'Ajman, Shaikh Hameed bin Rashid al Nu'aimi; the Crown Prince of Umm al-Quwain, Shaikh Rashid bin Ahmad al-Mu'alla; in addition to the children of the deceased, his brothers and cousins; and a large number of their Highnesses, the Shaikhs; their Excellencies, the ministers and the heads of the diplomatic missions; and a huge crowd of citizens.

In addition to an obituary statement made by the *Diwan* of the Ruler of Sharjah, a statement from the Cabinet of Ministers was also issued, and the weekly Cabinet meeting was cancelled.

The Election of the Speaker of the Federal National Council

On Tuesday 1 March 1977, Taryam bin Imran was elected as the Speaker of the National Federal Council. Taryam had been my best friend. We shared political activism, hopes and thoughts. We were together from early school days till we graduated from university. He graduated from the Sociology Department of Cairo University in 1968, and I from the Faculty of Agriculture in 1971. The three-year period during which we had gone our separate ways was when I worked as a teacher in the Industrial School in Sharjah. Taryam worked as Head of the Social Affairs Department in Sharjah just before the rule of the late Ruler of Sharjah, HH Shaikh Khalid bin Muhammad al-Qasimi. Together with his brother Abdullah, Taryam founded the first daily newspaper in the country, *al-Khaleej*, in addition to the first weekly magazine, *al-Shorooq*. Both publications appeared in 1968. He was also the UAE Ambassador to Egypt from the foundation of the Federation, and was the UAE representative in the League of Arab States.

He played an active role in the Arab-European Dialogue, and chaired its session of 1975 in Abu Dhabi. HH Shaikh Zayed bin Sultan Al Nahyan and the members of the Supreme Council attended the inauguration. The President of the State gave a speech in that session stating,

> Our call is that of unity. The goal we have set for ourselves that is dearest to our hearts is establishing an Arab unity that goes beyond this region – a region that shares a common history, that has the same aspirations, and that has the same visions for the future. We are against all types of division and strongly support true unity in every part of the Arab homeland. We desire peace for ourselves and others. We seek safety and security for our region and everywhere else in the world. We wish for stability for our people and the peoples of the world. We want prosperity for our nation and the future generations as well as for the whole of humanity.

The Meeting of the Arab Committee for Female Scouts

On Tuesday 1 March 1977, I inaugurated the Arab Committee for Female Scouts and gave a speech in which I announced that the State would do everything it could to accomplish the goals of the female Scouts.

The First Girl Scouts Team in the UAE was formed in January 1973. It had five hundred members and participated in the first Scouts camp in Hamriya.

I had sponsored the Sharjah Girl Scouts Authority both financially and spiritually since its inception as it was an integrated educational movement aimed at fostering the practice of good citizenship in all aspects.

In 1975, nine Girl Leaders went out of the Emirates for the first time to attend the training course held by the Arab Office for Girl Scouts in Bahrain.

In the same year the Girl Scouts Authority attended the Cairo Meeting of the Arab Committee for Girl Scouts, and the Emirates Girl Scouts Authority was accepted as a member in the Meeting.

In 1976, the Girl Scouts Authority participated in the Fourth Conference for Girl Scouts in Tunisia, where it was officially accepted as a member in the Arab Office. By the time of the conference, the number of members was 1,675 guides and junior members. The building used now as headquarters for the Girl Scouts Authority was a gift from me to them, and it was formerly the headquarters of the Emiri Diwan in al-Fayhaa district.

Visits to Syria and Saudi Arabia

On the morning of Friday 18 March 1977, I made an official visit to Syria for four days, during which I met the Syrian President Hafiz al-Asad. I also visited the front line at al-Qunaitra, between Syria and Israel, and then toured a number of factories and museums. My next official visit in that year was to Saudi Arabia.

On the morning of Tuesday 17 May 1977, I landed in Riyadh for a one-day visit to congratulate King Khalid bin 'Abdul-'Aziz al-Su'ud on his safe return after a successful trip to obtain medical treatment. At our reception was the Governor of Riyadh, HRH Prince Salman bin 'Abdul-'Aziz al-Su'ud.

In a meeting with King Khalid bin 'Abdul-'Aziz al-Su'ud, and in the presence of HRH Crown Prince Fahd bin 'Abdul-'Aziz, I expressed the appreciation of the UAE's President and its people for the Kingdom of Saudi Arabia and its government.

9

Putting the State Budget in Order

IN THE MEETING OF THE Supreme Council of the Federation held on 6 November 1976, the Ministerial Committee for Financial Affairs submitted to the Council a general budget proposed for the year 1977. The estimates in the budget were very high and there was a need for a re-examination of its contents. A committee had to be formed to this end in charge of discussing and determining the framework of the proposed 1977 budget in light of the needs presented by the Federal ministries and agencies. HH Shaikh Rashid bin Sa'id al-Maktoum, the Vice-President, suggested to the President of the State, Shaikh Zayed bin Sultan Al Nahyan, that I chair that committee. The members of the committee were HH Shaikh Hamad bin Muhammad al-Sharqi, Ruler of al-Fujairah, and HH Shaikh Hameed bin Rashid al-Nu'aimi, Crown Prince of 'Ajman, in addition to the members of the Ministerial Committee for Financial Affairs. I accepted the suggestion that I chair the committee in spite of my extremely busy schedule at the time with the aforementioned meetings and other events. I started my work by holding discussions about the budgets of the various ministries and institutions. This went on every week for four months. The aim was not only to determine the amount of the funds required, but to reform the State's financial and administrative systems as well. I studied all the systems in force in the governmental system.

On 7 May 1977, the Supreme Budget Committee submitted the budget proposal for the year 1977 to the National Federal Council in preparation for its discussion in the session that was to be held for this purpose. The most important points in the budget proposal were: making available the required funds for about 4,000 jobs not covered in previous budgets; creating about 5,000 new and needed jobs which would increase the number of Federal employees to a total of 34,000; and putting in place a new pay scale with incentives and encouragements for State employees which were intended to meet new living conditions in the UAE. According to the proposed scale, produced by the committee during its final meetings in early May 1977, the basic salaries were to be raised by 40 per cent with a minimum increase of AED 450 per month and a maximum of AED 1,500 per month. The total amount provided for in the State's General Budget for the year 1977 was about AED 11 billion.

On Tuesday 18 May 1977 and Saturday 9 June 1977 respectively, the National Council and the Federal Supreme Council approved the aforementioned budget.

Speech at the Federal National Council: Transparency and Accountability

On the morning of Tuesday 21 June 1977, I met with HH Shaikh Zayed bin Sultan Al Nahyan, President of the State, and informed him that I was going to deliver a speech in the National Federal Council after our meeting. I explained to HH Shaikh Zayed the contents of my speech. HH Shaikh Zayed approved of my speech.

I delivered my speech before the Council, and after greeting everyone I said:

Dear Brothers, Members of the Federal National Council, I would like to start by thanking you for the generous invitation to me to address this esteemed Council.

I was looking forward to this meeting with you as my dear Brothers, in whose abilities I have every confidence and hope. I have followed your deliberations in this Council in heart and mind as I believe that objective discussions are a must for the sake of achieving our ultimate aim free from bias or the need to serve personal interests. This is where true democracy is manifested.

Please allow me to address you today in all frankness, laying facts bare and clear so that you can approach them with right mindset. All of you, by the same token, have been entrusted with the affairs of this country and need to be made aware of all issues. I direct you to fulfil this trust before Allah, in the name of our heritage, our people and the Arab nation.

Our country, the UAE, believing in unification as the right path forward, has taken giant steps on the way to development and progress in spite of all the difficulties encountered. The whole world testifies to this.

We lived divided previously, engaged in continual disputes – and hatred was omnipresent in our midst. We had been separated from the Arab nation for many years. However, owing to your sincere efforts, good intentions and strong determination, our will to be united won the day. Obstacles have been overcome and the State has been established.

When the United Arab Emirates gained its unity and independence, opposing powers, Britain and Iran for example, believed that success and unity were goals too distant for the likes of us to reach. Such powers worked hard to widen the breaches between the various Emirates and families. They even succeeded in driving a wedge between oneself and one's own brother. They wanted hate, spite and malice to reign supreme and they waited to reap the fruit of their debased actions.

Those powers had also cast doubts on the abilities of the sons and daughters of this country. They also left *agents provocateurs* behind who conspired against this country – a country which had harboured no ill towards anyone nor had discriminated against any other because of race or place of origin.

This country had for so long been afflicted by foreigners who squandered its resources over a long period of time and who continually trafficked illicitly in our country's honour, assets and economy.

However, our ship managed to sail on and is now being piloted by a wise captain – a leader who made the historical decision during the Ramadan/October war (1973) to effect an oil embargo against the enemies of the Arabs at a time when hesitation and fear were at their peak; a leader who proclaimed 'Arab oil is not more precious than Arab blood', a dictum that found its way to the very heart of millions of Arabs; a leader who now finds himself at the helm of this country, the engineer of its renaissance.

Dear Brothers, it is no secret that I am one of the greatest advocates of unification. Once, in 1973, I said to HH Shaikh Zayed, President of the State, that this country had to be united. He wisely responded saying, 'Do not jump ahead of time. With time shall come the desired unity.' And here we are, after all that time and after all the difficult choices we had to make – we have, indeed, taken the necessary steps towards unity.

It is your right that all facts be brought into the open, especially after we have shown a great deal of tolerance towards many who were not worthy of our trust. We have not been like this because of weakness or complacency on our part; rather, it is the predisposition of this country to be generous and forgiving. However, we need to reveal wrongdoing, since henceforth we shall no longer tolerate the actions of those who abuse this country in any shape or form. We shall deter offenders at all costs. Some people have had the mistaken idea that Federation afforded the opportunity to loot and plunder, or to work for one's personal interests or regional gains. It is my understanding and belief, however, that Federation means sacrifice, generosity, sincerity, loyalty and love for this dear country.

Brothers, I should like to move on to address another issue, that of the Supreme Budget Committee.

When the proposed budget was submitted to the Supreme Council towards the end of last year, it was too big to implement. Therefore, the Supreme Council appointed a committee to examine the budget anew. We started the work, and, already in the first week, we realised that we were floundering in an ocean of problems. Some of them were as follows:

- There were misunderstandings between all the ministries on one side, and the Ministry of Finance on the other side. The latter was viewed as very strict in allowing expenditure to the extent that other ministries perceived this as being a case of mistrust. This was due to the lack of a regulatory mechanism to govern the relationship between both sides;
- There was also another kind of misunderstanding between all the ministries and the Council of Civil Service in charge of recruitment. Once again, there was nothing there to govern the relationship between the two;
- Inadequate, absent and/or inefficient laws led to the disruption of many projects; and
- The pay scale for ministry employees was very low in comparison with the private sector. This had led to an atmosphere of indifference and carelessness. However, we have all witnessed rapid growth in our country in addition to the change around us in world conditions. This obliged certain ministries to apply for an increase in the salaries of their employees because of consumer price increases and/or in comparison with the salaries of their peers in neighbouring

countries and/or because of the ministries' need to retain experienced employees in the various fields of those ministries' endeavours.

As a result, the Cabinet of Ministers approved the pay scales for each of these public sectors: education; health; pharmacists and veterinarians; mosque Imams and *Muezzins*; the police; the army.

This had negative consequences since other sectors and professions felt left out. The level of service and productivity deteriorated. This was in clear violation of Article 119 of Federal Law No. 8 (1973).

This situation necessitated that controls be introduced before submission of the budget. The committee, therefore, decided to examine a number of areas including the following: the Civil Service system; Job classifications; the Accounting/ Auditing system; Tenders and Auctions Law; and Statutes dealing with Stores Procurement and Warehousing.

As for the system of the Civil Service, the committee considered adopting the system of the Employees' *Diwan* or reforming the existing Civil Service system. After lengthy discussions, the committee approved amending the current system and adding some articles for two main reasons. First, the Civil Service system was already in existence and all civil servants are familiar with it. Second, the Civil Service Law governs what already exists, while the Employees' *Diwan* is not enforceable yet.

The committee has also highlighted other issues that needed urgent solutions. For job classifications, for example, the qualifications, requirement or conditions for employment were non-existent. We came to hear that an engineer in a certain ministry was earning a salary twice as much as an engineer with the same qualifications and years of experience in another ministry. Jobs were therefore reclassified according to academic qualifications and practical experience, though this proviso did not apply to our own nationals. As for the Accounting/Auditing system, the committee decided to postpone discussions till the first session after the summer in order not to disrupt related work. As for the Tenders and Auctions Law, each ministry presented its purchasing system and procedures. Regarding the corpus of Stores Procurement and warehousing statutes, this is an administrative process meant to govern the rules and regulations in relation to stored items and conducting an inventory of all the items in order to avoid wasteful duplicate purchasing.

In light of the above, a number of observations could be concluded: firstly, and regarding the Civil Service system, there is desperate need for cooperation between the Service Council and the ministries and for controls to regulate their inter-relationship. Secondly, and regarding laws of tendering, auctions and direct purchases, certain powers need to be vested in each ministry in cooperation with the Ministry of Finance and in order to engage in tendering, auctions and direct purchasing.

As for the budget, I will not deal with it here as His Excellency, the Minister of Finance, has already explained its different articles. I also understand that some of the Brother members of the Council made certain observations, among which are: firstly, the budget delay. This was due to the fact that the ministries were not yet well versed in using the new procedures in the budget discussions with the committee this year. Secondly, the size of the new projects. There have been a number of projects on hold for years, and they have been awaiting completion because the capacity of the Ministry of Works to execute projects was much smaller than what the ministry could undertake. Therefore, all incomplete projects from the years 1974, 1975 and 1976 were grouped together to be completed in one year.

Brothers, I must now move to another issue of great importance, and there is a need that it be addressed openly.

I am sure you will agree with me that scientific planning for our State represents the future outlook as to what this country is to become. This has to be based on knowledge and sound planning. There is indeed a need for light and heavy industries, manpower, establishing a future vision for agricultural development as well as industrial, cultural and social development. All this requires proper planning. We also need to identify what projects are needed within a specific number of years, and so on.

It is a well-known fact that no country can properly function without proper planning based on actual needs. The plan should start with a vision of the future, and then establish a mechanism for the implementation of the plan within a defined period of time. To have a vision, there is need for a Supreme Council for National Planning whose job is to plan and follow up the implementation of the various phases of such a plan. It should also be able to revise the stages, determine what is right and wrong, rethink issues and put things back on the right track, and so on.

If you consider the UAE as a living exemplar, you will note a population of 650,000 people, 250,000 of whom are nationals and the rest Arab and foreign expatriates. So, what could our plans be for industrialisation in such a case? If we were to plan to increase industrialisation in the UAE, this would then require an increase in the percentage of expatriates against that of our own nationals.

Some may ask, 'Is there really any danger if this were to happen?' I can answer this question by saying that there is a solution for every situation. However, the danger in our situation is more on the social side since Emirati nationals will continue to remain a minority for a few years yet. Another side to this problem is that, if we plan for more projects, a different type of percentage will be affected. Currently, the ratio of males to females in the UAE is 5:1. So, we need to reckon what this percentage is going to be should we bring even more expatriates in for our new industries. In other words, an advance study for any project is required beforehand. This will be an advantage that we cannot underestimate.

Another example in relation to manpower and recruitment is that of the raw materials that could be used to establish a manufacturing industry that does not require a large workforce. Proper planning will help us deal with this issue based on actual need. It is an indisputable fact that our country lacks raw materials. However, we have plenty of energy which we could use as the basis for petrochemical industries where manpower is not required in large quantities. This would be another advantage that accrues because of well-informed planning – and there are, indeed, many others.

Brothers, I should like to conclude by thanking you all for listening. I wish to reiterate that we have great confidence in you and are ever hopeful that you will achieve all that is needed. At the same time, you are required, more than ever before, to maintain the unity and integrity of this State. You have to raise your voices for incorporation and unity. This is indeed our message and it should be yours in your capacity as the Supreme Legislative Body. It is also the message of our mass media which has an important role to play in stressing our Arab and Islamic identity: we are an Arab and Muslim country in terms of our constitution; and our values need to be translated into reality in our schools, clubs and society. This is a message we all have to communicate in all faithfulness, honesty, sincerity and dedication.

May Allah guide you all to what is best for our nation, and my wishes for success go to the National Council under the guidance of the President of the State, HH Shaikh Zayed bin Sultan Al Nahyan. Thank you.

Budget and Policies

Once I had finished my speech, questions and inquiries started to flow from members of the Federal National Council. The first question came from Naser Lutah, who wanted to know what the State's policy was regarding foreigners owning land and property in the UAE and what regulations governed this particular issue, especially considering that there were many instances where foreigners purchased property, established projects on them, then sold them on to nationals. After doing so, they returned to their countries, creating a cash flow problem in the UAE.

'There is a committee,' I said,

that the Cabinet has formed to investigate issues such as those related to internal security and economic aspects, with particular emphasis on the commercial projects that include foreign national parties. This committee also deals with issues of land owned by non-nationals and those dealing with the coordination of industrial projects. The Supreme Council has discussed such issues and proper measures have been taken which included that the Minister of the Interior was commissioned to ensure that no expatriate workers over the age of fifty be recruited, and that they should be free from illness and should not be permitted to remain for more than twenty-four months. Also, the Supreme Council requested that the Labour Act be implemented and inspection campaigns be undertaken to determine the presence of illegal residents. In parallel to that the Cabinet spin-off committee was asked to come up with a proposal determining a means of ensuring that foreigners do not own property and that nationals are not party to related issues of trade. This committee will establish contact with Kuwait, Saudi Arabia and Qatar to benefit from their experience with laws that relate to this issue. As for industrialisation, the Minister of Planning was commissioned to prepare a State inventory and develop a plan to ensure that no conflicts in terms of industrial projects in the country occurred.

The next question was from a member, Ahmad Sultan al-Jaber, about the provisional constitution which was in force until then in spite of the fact that the Supreme Council had already made a decision to form a committee to look into the issue of the permanent constitution. When the aforementioned committee had finished its task, the permanent constitution issue was postponed and even the provisional constitution had not been 100 per cent implemented.

My response was:

This State was established at a time when we were divided. The opponents of the commonwealth and the public interest are still out there, working on stirring up more trouble. When it dealt with our unity, HH Shaikh Zayed said that, with time, our goal would be realised. We need to compare how we were two years ago, and where we stand today. I can confirm that 90 per cent of our Federal goals have been realised. The Departments of Security, Defence, Mass Media and local institutions have all been incorporated. This has been achieved in a relatively short period of time. I recall one of the brothers asking HH Shaikh Zayed in Cairo saying, 'How could there be a dispute between Cairo and Alexandria?',[16] to which Shaikh Zayed responded, 'Tell me when Cairo and Alexandria became unified, and then I will give you my answer.'

I had mentioned in my address that when I asked the Shaikh about the importance of being one unified body, he said that it

---

[16] Hinting at some disputes between individual emirates.

was important not to run ahead of time, and that, with time, comes unity.

I then added:

It is true that there are benefits in having a permanent constitution. However, such benefits will cease to exist beyond the stage of unification if consensus on all articles of the permanent constitution is not realised. The provisional constitution, on the other hand, allows us to take the much needed time to prepare for unity without being bogged down by constitutional phraseology.

I have always been a strong advocate of a permanent constitution. Yet, I have come to realise that it has as many factors leading to unity as those hindering the achievement of a sustainable unity. As a result, the Supreme Council has decided to postpone its deliberations in this regard so that a longer period might be invested in discussing the important issues. My belief is that if the new constitution is going to restrict us, then it is better not to cling to it. And if the provisional constitution is allowing us to work more freely, then it is much better to continue working to incorporate into the provisional constitution those elements that lead to our ultimate unity.

I then concluded, saying, 'As for the current problems, we hope that they are only temporary and that they will have no impact on how we feel or on the course the State is taking. Our country needs those who love her to be generous and giving. We certainly love our country and wish her the best.'

Ahmad Rahma al-Amri then asked, 'Your Highness, you said that the future of our country may not be realised without scientific planning; and stated that this may not be achieved except through a Supreme Council for Planning. Are there any steps that have been taken towards forming such a Council? And are you happy with the provisional constitution?'

'We are a Muslim State,' I said.

Many people are confused when we use the word constitution and mean legal statutes – since the true constitution is the Qur'an. Therefore, since we are a Muslim country, what we must abide by are the contents of the constitution, that is, the Qur'an.

As for whether I was happy with the provisional constitution, I can only say that it fulfils about 65–70 per cent of what we aspire to. The fear was that we may unwittingly waste the remaining 30 per cent of our unity goals.

As for the Planning Council, we have already been discussing the financial problems and the systems required, and have found that there is a need for comprehensive planning for every village in the country, which we ought to carry out since we want to stress the fact that we are all, indeed, one country.

We have found that there are sixty families in some villages living in only ten houses. There are also villages deprived of electricity and other services. That's why we have asked the Ministry of Planning to look at the map of the whole UAE, and create a Federal plan whose services will reach all villages so that we become aware of the living conditions in the country and the need for schools, hospitals and other services. Work is now progressing so that we can acquire a full picture of this issue.

The Supreme Budget Committee will check living conditions, and visit these villages and sites after the summer. In addition to preparing the budget, the committee will conduct inspection trips to every village with the Ministries of Planning, Works, Education and all relevant ministries to determine their needs and decide both what has been accomplished and what remains to be done.

Next year it will be shown that most projects will focus on the services that are needed in the villages and in Bedouin areas since they are very poor. The inhabitants of those places are more in need of help than those whose income per capita is enough to meet the requirements of a reasonable standard of living.

Hamad bu Shihab asked, 'Your Highness, you can see that the State budget expenditure is centralised in the hands of the Ministry of Finance. We have also noticed that, in the past five years, ministers who come to the Council to discuss their own ministries' businesses complain that the Ministry of Finance is always the cause of problems. I should like, furthermore, to ask about the incorporation of the Security Departments. Does this really mean incorporation, all in one, or coordination? Thirdly, what is happening with the Law of Commercial Agencies? We can see that such agencies are owned by foreigners in 99.9 per cent of the cases. Lastly, what are the criteria followed in setting up the new pay scales?'

I replied:

There seems to be a lot of misunderstanding when speaking about the Ministry of Finance. I was personally among those who had criticised its work before I found out that the problem was the lack of rules and regulations that govern the relation between it and the other ministries. What exactly happened was that the Ministry, by its very nature, had to be very strict. When you are entrusted with another's finances, then you must be very cautious not to waste what you have been entrusted with. The Ministry is very wary of overspending; and, by the same token, certain ministers complained that they did not have the power to spend even as little as AED 5,000.

Now, after setting up controls that govern the relationship with the Ministry of Finance, and giving the ministers sufficient powers – to the extent that some of them have said they are happy with 50 per cent of what has been achieved through the Supreme Committee – I can say that no one, after today, will come to complain about the Ministry of Finance or the Service Council.

As for the Law of Agencies, I have mentioned that, as one of the tasks of the Cabinet spin-off committee, it will look into how neighbouring countries have been dealing with this issue. As regards the police, well, I know that the Police Force is totally Federal in all its affairs, spending and procedures.

Regarding the pay scales, they are available to you for examination. I also heard that there was a proposal to reduce the maximum level and to raise the minimum. I should note that in increasing the salaries of civil servants, the increases do not apply to all employees such as those working for the police or the army, or to doctors, teachers and veterinarians. Those professions have received increases all the time to the extent that other civil servants felt unjustly treated, although they were the working machinery of the government and the very ones who were charged with the responsibility of dealing with all the State problems. As a result of this, there was a sense of carelessness and indifference which led to cases of embezzlement, bribery and other matters that were alien to our society and totally unacceptable. I personally do not doubt the honesty of any civil servant, but carelessness and inefficiency at work have caused many projects to come to a halt and a reduction in our normal rate of achievement.

It was therefore necessary to study the standard of living in the UAE and compare this to that of Qatar, Saudi Arabia and Kuwait. We looked into the pay scales in these countries and found out that some of them took our pay scale and gradually over the years doubled it, while we were at a standstill. In Saudi Arabia, we find that living expenses are low as the State subsidises many of the items. In Kuwait, there are cooperatives which sell essential goods at reduced prices. As for our pay scale, it is not only related to finances as some may think. So, we have endeavoured to take it to a reasonable level.

10

Zayed in Tehran

IN OCTOBER 1977 HH SHAIKH Zayed bin Sultan Al Nahyan received an official invitation from Shah Mohammad Reza Pahlavi to visit Iran. HH Shaikh Zayed accepted the invitation, and 1 November 1977 was set as a date for the visit.

The Shah asked me to come to Iran before Shaikh Zayed's visit, following a conversation he had with my friend Kim Roosevelt. Mr Roosevelt was the US intelligence officer in the region at the time when Mohammad Mosaddegh had been elected Prime Minister and had nationalised the Iran oil industry in 1951. After Shah Pahlavi had fled Iran after Mosaddegh's election, Roosevelt managed to restore the Shah to his throne in 1953.[17]

Before going to Iran to meet the Shah, Kim Roosevelt visited me in Sharjah, and I talked to him about Shaikh Zayed and his impending visit to Iran.

---

[17] Mosaddegh was overthrown in 1953 by an infamous CIA-organised coup after which the Shah was reinstated.

'Shaikh Zayed is a friend,' I said. 'I know him very well. The Shah, however, has been totally misinformed about him, and I wish that the Shah should consider Shaikh Zayed as a friend. So, it is imperative that Shaikh Zayed be welcomed in Tehran to demonstrate that the Shah has changed the view he formerly had of Shaikh Zayed.'[18]

Prior to my travelling to Iran, I planned official visits to Yemen and Sudan which I shall now discuss before turning back to the visit to Iran.

After President Ibrahim al-Hamdi visited Sharjah on 20 December 1976 on his way to Beijing, he invited me to Yemen at a date to be decided later. The visit was finally arranged for the second half of October 1977. But President al-Hamdi was assassinated on 12 October 1977, and consequently my visit did not materialise. The Sudan visit was also proposed earlier on but had been postponed the previous year following the executions that were carried out at the time. However, new arrangements were eventually finalised, and we started our visit on 22 October 1977. The delegates accompanying me were: His Excellency Shaikh Ahmad bin Sultan al-Qasimi, Minister of State; His Excellency Hamouda bin Ali al-Zaheri, Minister of State for Internal Affairs; His Excellency Abdullah bin Imran bin Taryam, Minister of Education and Youth; His Excellency Taryam bin Imran bin Taryam, Speaker of the National Federal Council; and Mr Sultan al-Suwaidi, Director of Ceremonies in Sharjah.

When we landed, our reception at Khartoum airport was

---

[18] See Chapter 1 for details.

headed by First Vice-President, Mr Abul-Qasem Muhammad Ibrahim, Mr al-Rasheed Taher Bakr, and a number of ministers and high officials in the Sudanese government.

During our visit, in addition to meeting President Jaafar Nimeiry we also visited the Jazeera agricultural project.

Visit to Iran

Together with my accompanying delegates, I flew from Khartoum to Tehran on 25 October 1977, where a number of Iranian officials met our delegation at the airport. Later on, and during the meeting with the Shah in his palace, I spoke to him about Shaikh Zayed, and I asked: 'Did you meet Kim Roosevelt?'

Smiling, the Shah said 'Yes, I did. And what are you asking for your friend [Shaikh Zayed]?'

'All due respect and a very warm welcome,' I said.

'Talk to Nussairi [Head of the Iranian Intelligence Agency, SAVAK], and he will arrange for all you ask,' the Shah said.

Afterwards, we left his office and the Shah walked with me to his car, and even opened the door himself for me. Then he took me on a tour of the palace complex – the office where we had met was at one side of it.

We reached the *majlis* where my delegates were waiting. After the Shah had exchanged greetings with them, we went to the dining area. As the rice was being served, His Excellency Hamouda bin Ali al-Zaheri took a grain of rice and started measuring it against his index finger. The Shah noticed this and said, 'This kind is long grain, which can easily break during cooking. But there is a special way of cooking it to prevent this from happening. Simply, all you need to do is to put the rice in warm water, then on low heat. When it has boiled, you drain it.'

His Excellency Hamouda bin Ali al-Zaheri responded saying, 'The Rice of the King is the King of all Rice'.

That evening, Prime Minister Amouzegar invited us for a dinner banquet. To my right at the table was Mr Nussairi, who informed me that the Shah had appointed him to discuss with me all the special arrangements regarding Shaikh Zayed's visit to Tehran.

'What arrangements will be made for someone like Shaikh Zayed?' I asked.

'The same as for any other Head of State,' Nussairi answered.

'What do you do that is more elaborate than that kind of reception?' I asked.

'The reception of the Shah upon his return from official visits or when he travels away for the same purpose,' Nussairi replied.

'Describe that for me,' I continued.

'After the official greeting and parade by the guards of honour, the Shah rides on a golden carriage drawn by white horses. To the right and left of the carriage, there are a hundred and fifty horse riders. The cavalcade proceeds until it reaches Shahabad Ariamehr Square, where young women perform traditional dancing, while holding incense burners,' explained Nussairi.

'I want exactly that ceremony for the reception of Shaikh Zayed,' I said.

'What? If I were to make such arrangements, those who had previously come to visit Iran would be angry, and those who will come later will demand the same.'

'You ask the Shah about what I have requested. If he says no, then anything he does for his guest is his business.'

Mr Nussairi left and after a short while he returned. Pressing my right hand, he said: 'The Shah has approved what you've asked for.'

I returned to Sharjah from Tehran on Friday 28 October 1977. Waiting for me were the details of the atrocity that had claimed the life of the Minister of Foreign Affairs, Saif bin Ghabbash, at Abu Dhabi airport.

On that day, the Syrian Foreign Minister, Mr Abdul-Halim Khaddam, had been visiting Abu Dhabi, and His Excellency Saif bin Ghabbash had been in the reception committee. Mr Khaddam was the target of an assassination, but Foreign Minister Ghabbash was the one who was hit and immediately killed.

I recalled, then, a private meeting with President Hafiz al-Asad of Syria. Upon my request the meeting was held on 21 March, on the last day of my official visit there, which started on 18 March 1977.

However, before I was able to give the reasons why I had requested the meeting with the President, Mr Khaddam entered the room, so I did not continue with what I wanted to say. After remaining silent for some time, I had to withdraw; therefore, I bade President al-Asad farewell and left.

Before leaving the guest house for the airport, a call came from the President, requesting that the procession leave for the airport together with Mr Khaddam, and that Shaikh Sultan al-Qasimi should return alone for a meeting with President al-Asad.

'Why did you not proceed with what you were saying when Abdul-Halim Khaddam came in?' President Asad asked.

'Because I was going to talk about Mr Khaddam himself,' I said.

'What about him?'

'When we visited Mr Khaddam in his office after our arrival in Damascus, he began swearing at and cursing Saddam Hussein and his group. He also made threats about occupying Baghdad in one hour. He also kept cursing Yasser Arafat and his Palestinian colleagues. This, Mr President, happened in the presence of a crowd of people including the delegates accompanying me. This kind of talk will not cause troubles for Mr Khaddam alone. Syria will be affected, too.' I then left him to ponder on what I had reported. It was ironic that Khaddam himself was about to be the target of an assassination by someone of Iraqi-Palestinian origin, and belonged to the people that he himself had threatened to kill. The assassin was arrested by our security forces.

Following the shooting at Abu Dhabi airport, emergency meetings of the Supreme Council and of the Cabinet of Ministers were called on 29 October 1977, and a statement from the Supreme Council of the Federation was issued saying, 'The responsibility of protecting the security of the country and the lives of the people requires that all requisite measures be taken to ensure this objective. The current situation also requires that perpetrators and outlaws be strongly deterred.' As the discussions of the Supreme Council of the Federation proceeded, it was revealed that the measures necessary for adequate security had not been sufficient.

Shaikh Zayed's Reception in Tehran

On the morning of Tuesday 1 November 1977, I was in the company of the members of the Supreme Council of the

Federation at Abu Dhabi airport to bid farewell to HH Shaikh Zayed bin Sultan Al Nahyan, President of the State, as he departed for his official visit to Iran. I then returned to Sharjah and waited for a long time for news of the official reception for HH Shaikh Zayed when he arrived in Tehran airport. I read the news the next day in the *al-Ittihād* newspaper. It said:

> Yesterday, Iran received its eminent guest, HH Shaikh Zayed bin Sultan Al Nahyan, President of the UAE. The official reception attracted huge crowds of people as Shaikh Zayed arrived in Tehran at 12.00 noon for a six-day visit. This was in response to an official invitation by His Imperial Majesty Mohammad Reza Pahlavi, Shah of Iran, who was personally at HH Shaikh Zayed's reception at Tehran International Airport, together with senior state officials, ministers and members of the Arab and foreign diplomatic corps in Iran.
>
> As the plane landed, His Excellency Eisa Khalfan, the UAE Ambassador to Tehran, went forward and escorted HH, the President of the State, as he descended the stairs from the plane to the runway where he was received by His Imperial Majesty Mohammad Reza Pahlavi, Shah of Iran. After a long hug, the two leaders had a brief, friendly chat; then a young girl came forward and presented HH, the great guest of Iran, with a floral tribute.
>
> Afterwards, HH, the President of the State, introduced his official delegates to His Majesty, the Shah of Iran. The Shah of Iran then introduced the senior officials at the reception.
>
> After greeting them, the President of the State went with the Shah to the VIP podium at Tehran airport whose entrances

and exits were decorated with the flags of the Emirates and Iran. The whole airport was also adorned with flowers everywhere. The national anthems of the two countries were also played. This was followed by a twenty-one-gun salute in honour of HH, the great guest of Iran. At the same time, seven jet fighters flew above in salutation. The two leaders then inspected a Guard of Honour comprised of about two hundred personnel.

Afterwards, the two leaders made their way back to the VIP podium where they watched a remarkable military display of seven minutes with military music mounted by the Guard of Honour in a circle around the podium. Then, HH, the President of the State, and the Shah shook hands with the members of the UAE Embassy in Tehran.

After the official ceremonies concluded at the airport, the procession of the two great leaders made its way to Shahabad Ariamehr Square in an Imperial carriage drawn by six white horses. The carriage was accompanied by four straight lines of more than 150 escorts mounted on black horses. The flags of the UAE decorated the road all the way to the Square. On both sides, the road was lined with crowds of people – there were both boy and girl school students, in addition to adult Iranian nationals, all holding the UAE flag in their hands and waving them in greeting for the great guest of Iran, HH Shaikh Zayed bin Sultan. The crowds, who were of all ages, were shouting welcoming greetings and everyone was happy and smiling. The cavalcade proceeded through the crowds that had been waiting from the early hours of the morning, in spite of the weather and the cold temperature of 12°C in the Iranian capital.

The two leaders disembarked from the royal carriage when they reached Shahabad Ariamehr Square, which is on a round, 20,000m² tract of land incorporating green squares, flowers, gardens and more than thirty water fountains. The Square, too, was swarming with crowds of Iranians who were greeted by the two leaders.

At the Square, a young Iranian boy and girl burned incense to greet HH, the President of the State, who, together with his brother, the Emperor Shah, walked to the memorial in the middle of the Square. On both sides of the road, groups of young people were clapping to welcome HH, the President of the State. At the memorial, Tehran's mayor delivered a welcome speech, and praised the good relations between the UAE and Iran. He then presented HH Shaikh Zayed with the 'Gift of the City', four silver kettles shaped as coffee-pots, which HH, the President of State, thankfully accepted.

From the Square, the two leaders headed for the Golestan Palace, where HH, President of the State, would be staying during his visit to Tehran.

The visit was considered by many to be a success. It resulted in improved relations and better understanding between the two countries.

Epilogue

THE SIXTH YEAR OF THE UAE State culminated with a precious gift from HH Shaikh Zayed bin Sultan Al Nahyan. This was his inauguration of the United Arab Emirates University, on Thursday 10 November 1977. In his speech for that occasion he said, 'The best investment is when money is dedicated to creating generations of well-educated people.' He added, 'It is time for us to restore our glory. This may not be done by means of money alone; rather, money has to be matched by the knowledge that guides planning, and provides enlightened minds to lead the way. Otherwise, money will perish and leave behind poverty and ignorance.'

On the morning of Monday 5 December 1977, the Supreme Council of the Federation convened under the chairmanship of HH Shaikh Zayed and was attended by their Highnesses, the Rulers of the Emirates. Some important decisions were made in support of the continued development of our Federal State, including the following: the Supreme Council gave the Ministry of the Interior wide powers to enhance security measures and control illegal immigration; local authorities were prevented from interfering in matters of naturalisation and residency; more studies were to be conducted regarding the reorganisation of the

Armed Forces; and the power of the Cabinet in the implementation of Federal laws, decrees and decisions throughout the country was strengthened.

These decisions were meant, in the first place, to support and stress the continued development of our Federal State.

At the beginning of 1978, a new budget of AED 10.5 billion was presented, and HH Shaikh Zayed approved an AED 50 million subsidy for foodstuff, to be implemented by the Supreme Budget Committee. HH Shaikh Zayed also decreed that housing allowance be paid to all citizens who had obtained public housing.

The Federation's path of development proceeded from strength to strength. When the Supreme Council of the Federation met on Monday 19 March 1979, the largest public march in the history of the country made its way to the capital, Abu Dhabi, where the meeting was taking place. The crowds were shouting for total integration and unity. His Highness, Shaikh Zayed, came out to them with tears of joy in his eyes and assured them, 'We will always maintain our march forward.'

Index of People

A Note on the Author

Born in 1939, Shaikh Sultan bin Muhammad al-Qasimi is the author of several books including *The Myth of Arab Piracy in the Gulf* (1986), *The Fragmentation of the Omani Empire* (1989), *The British Occupation of Aden* (1990) and the first volume of autobiography, *My Early Life* (2011).

A Note on the Type

The text of this book is set Adobe Garamond. It is one of several versions of Garamond based on the designs of Claude Garamond. It is thought that Garamond based his font on Bembo, cut in 1495 by Francesco Griffo in collaboration with the Italian printer Aldus Manutius. Garamond types were first used in books printed in Paris around 1532. Many of the present-day versions of this type are based on the *Typi Academiae* of Jean Jannon cut in Sedan in 1615.

Claude Garamond was born in Paris in 1480. He learned how to cut type from his father and by the age of fifteen he was able to fashion steel punches the size of a pica with great precision. At the age of sixty he was commissioned by King Francis I to design a Greek alphabet, for this he was given the honourable title of royal type founder. He died in 1561.